JUNGLE

Animals Coloring Book
For Kids

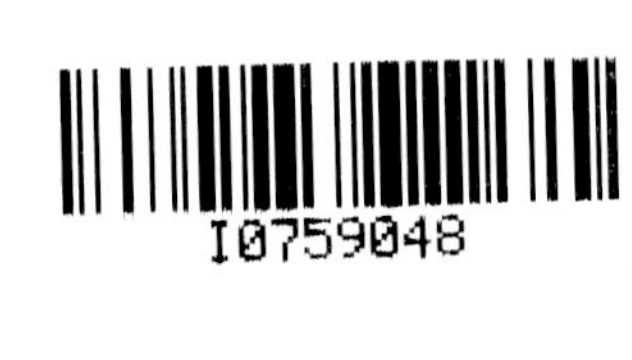

This Book Belongs To:

____

____

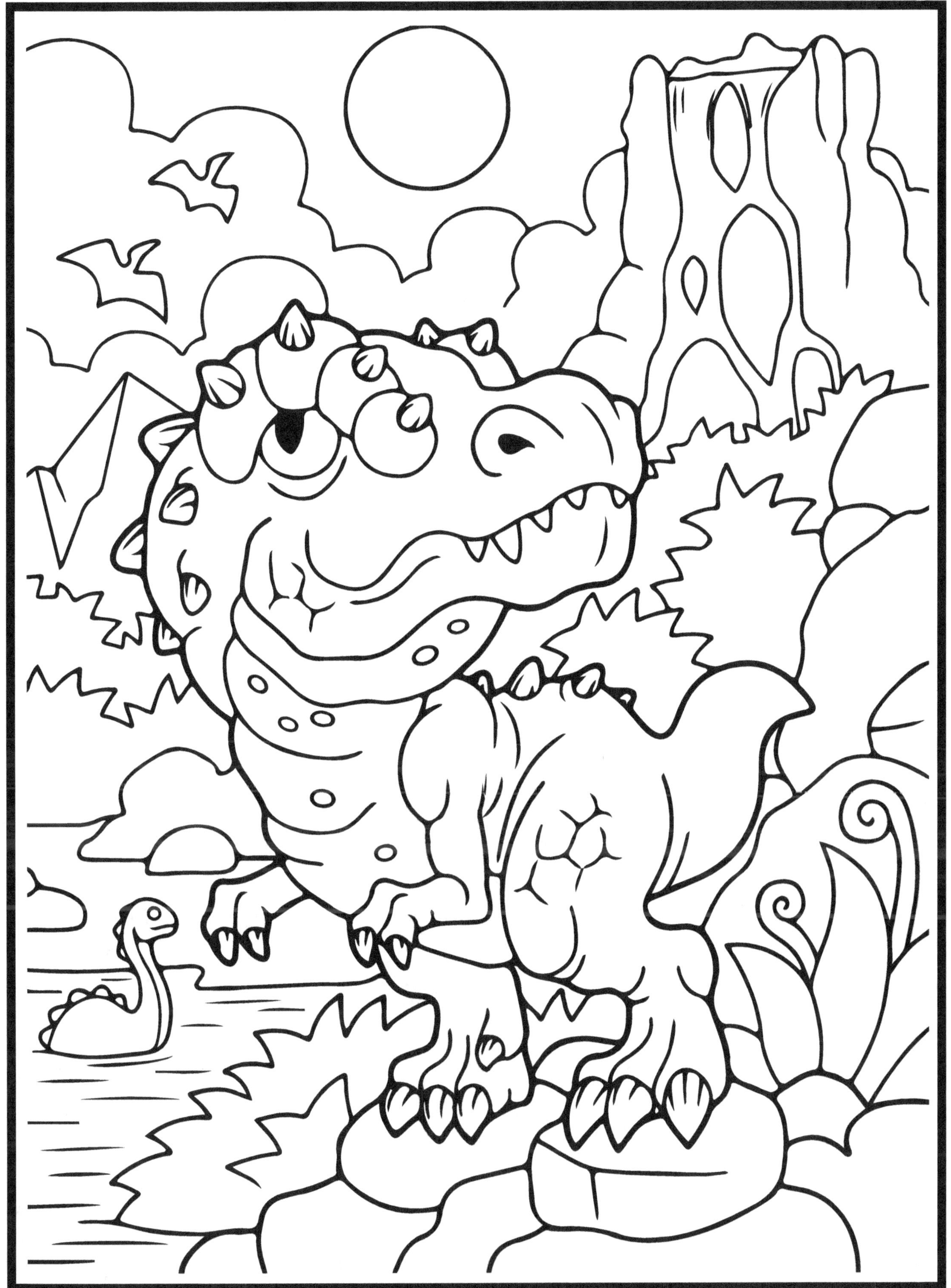

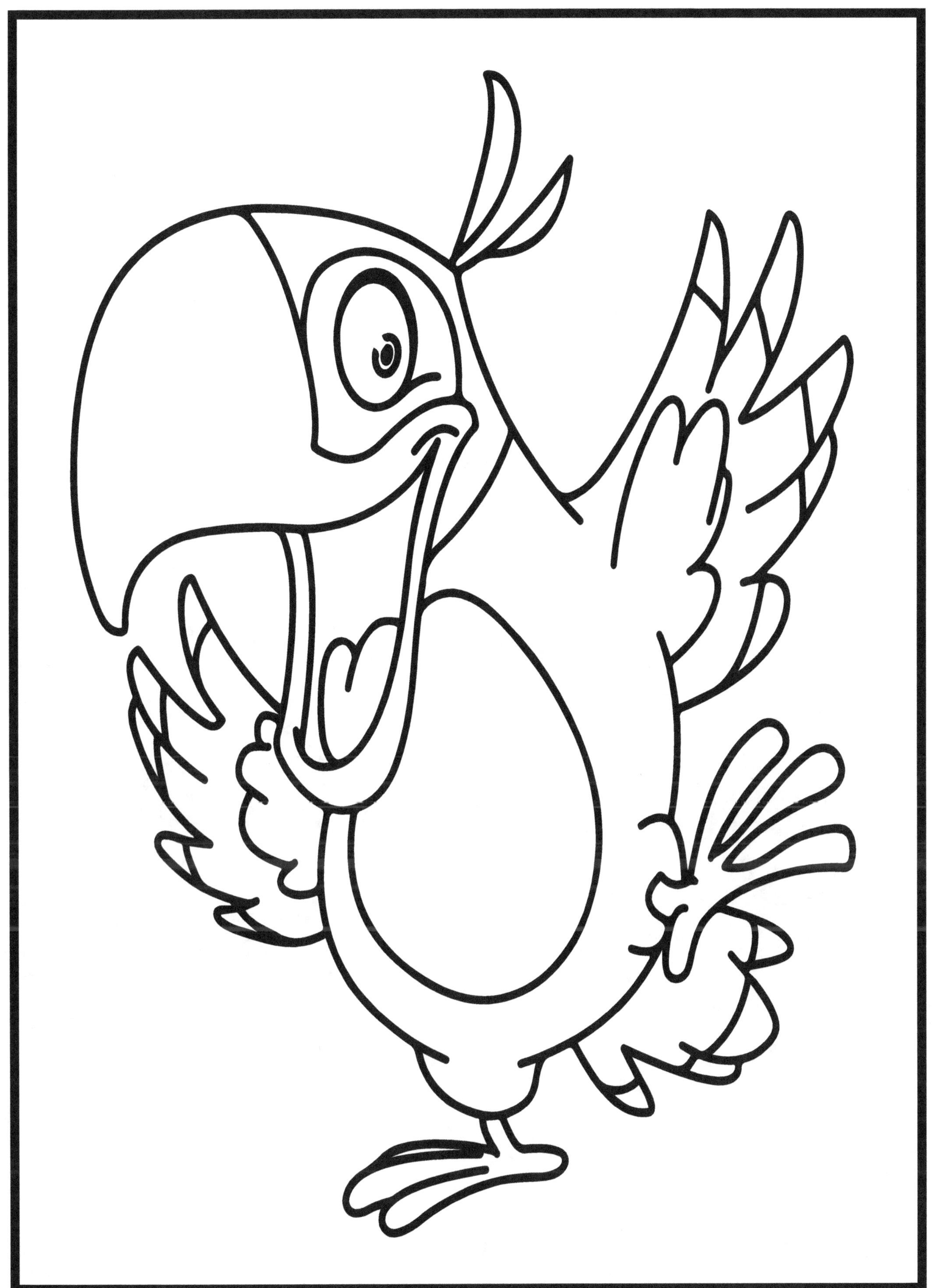

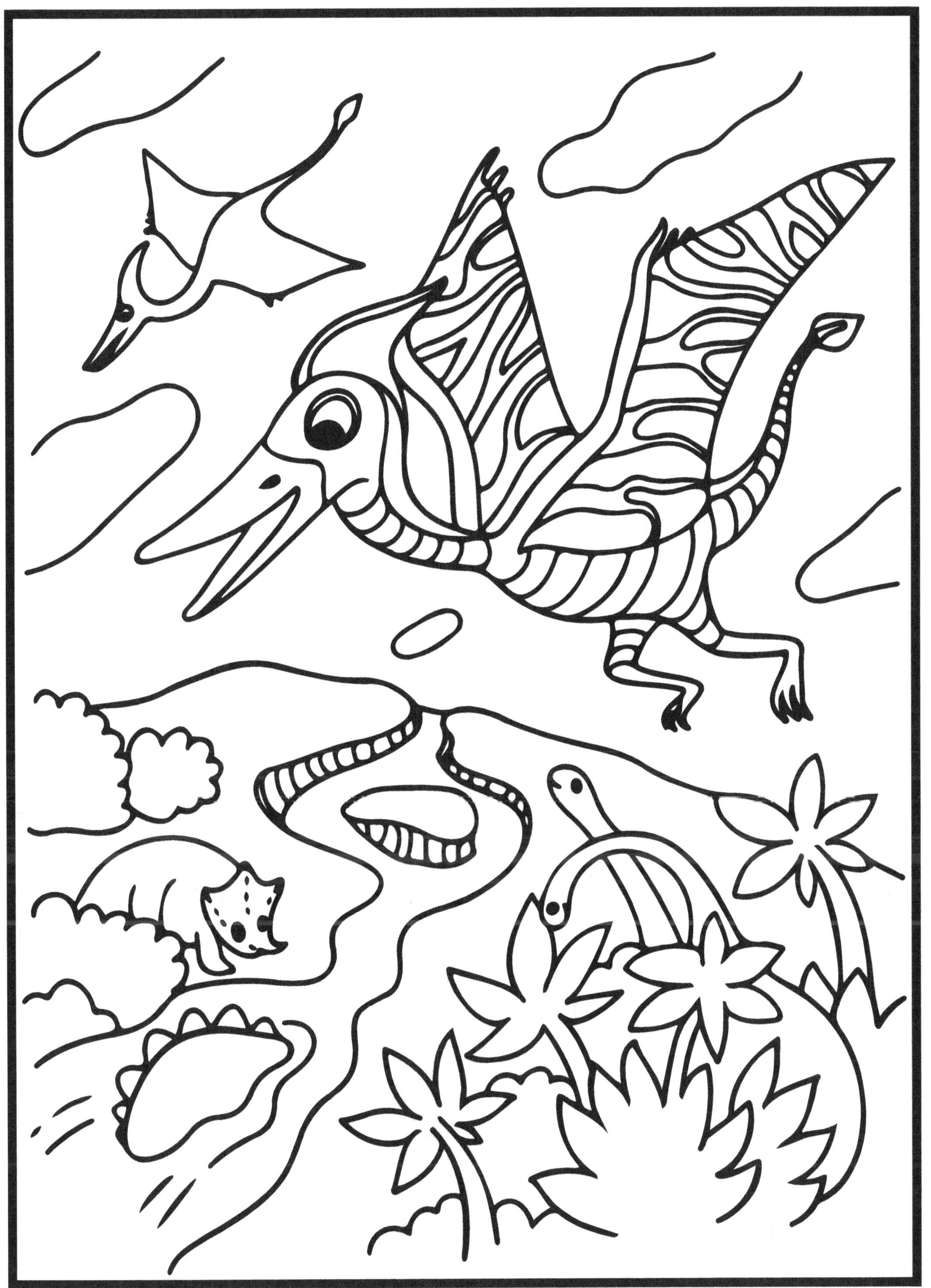

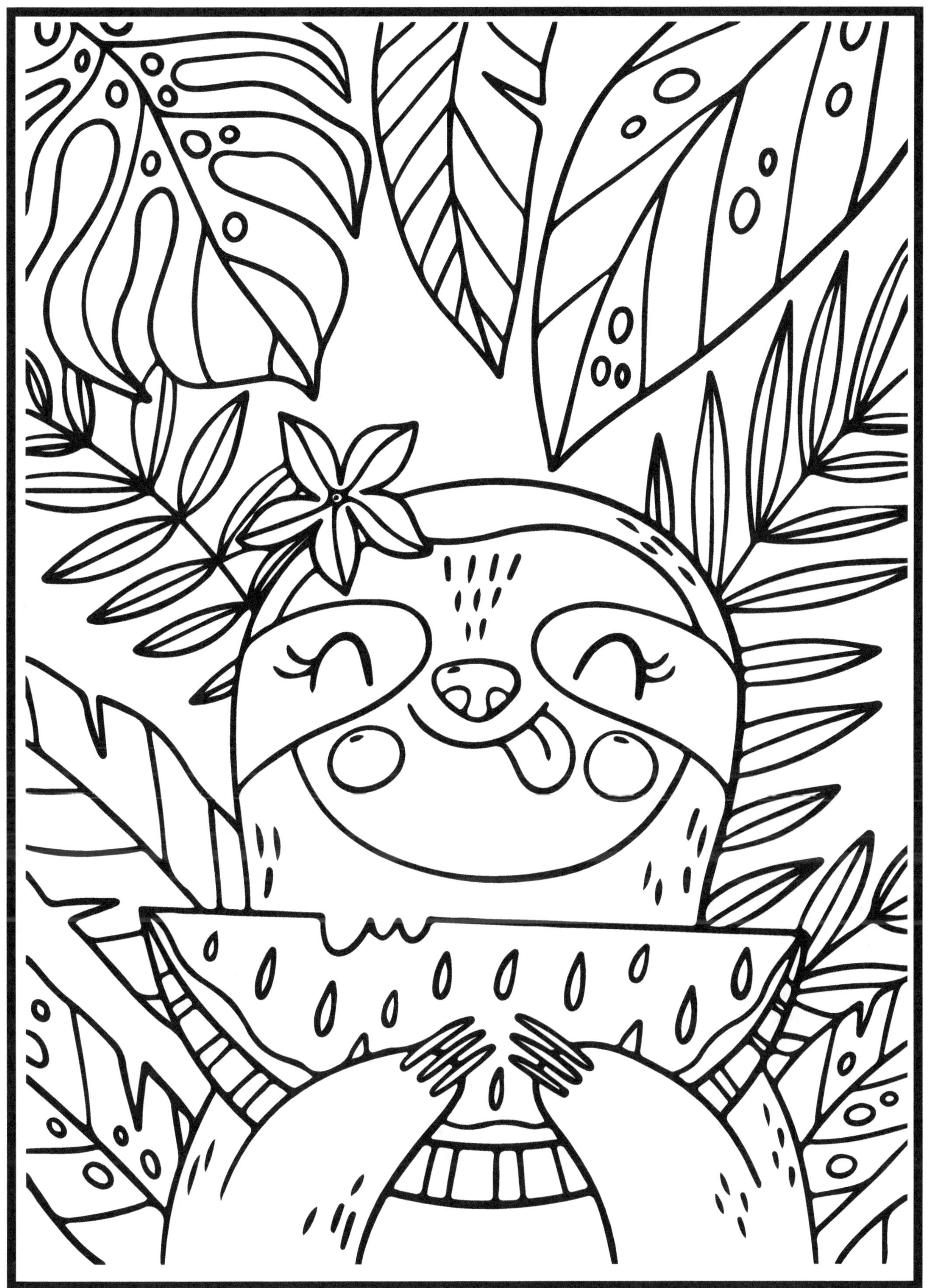

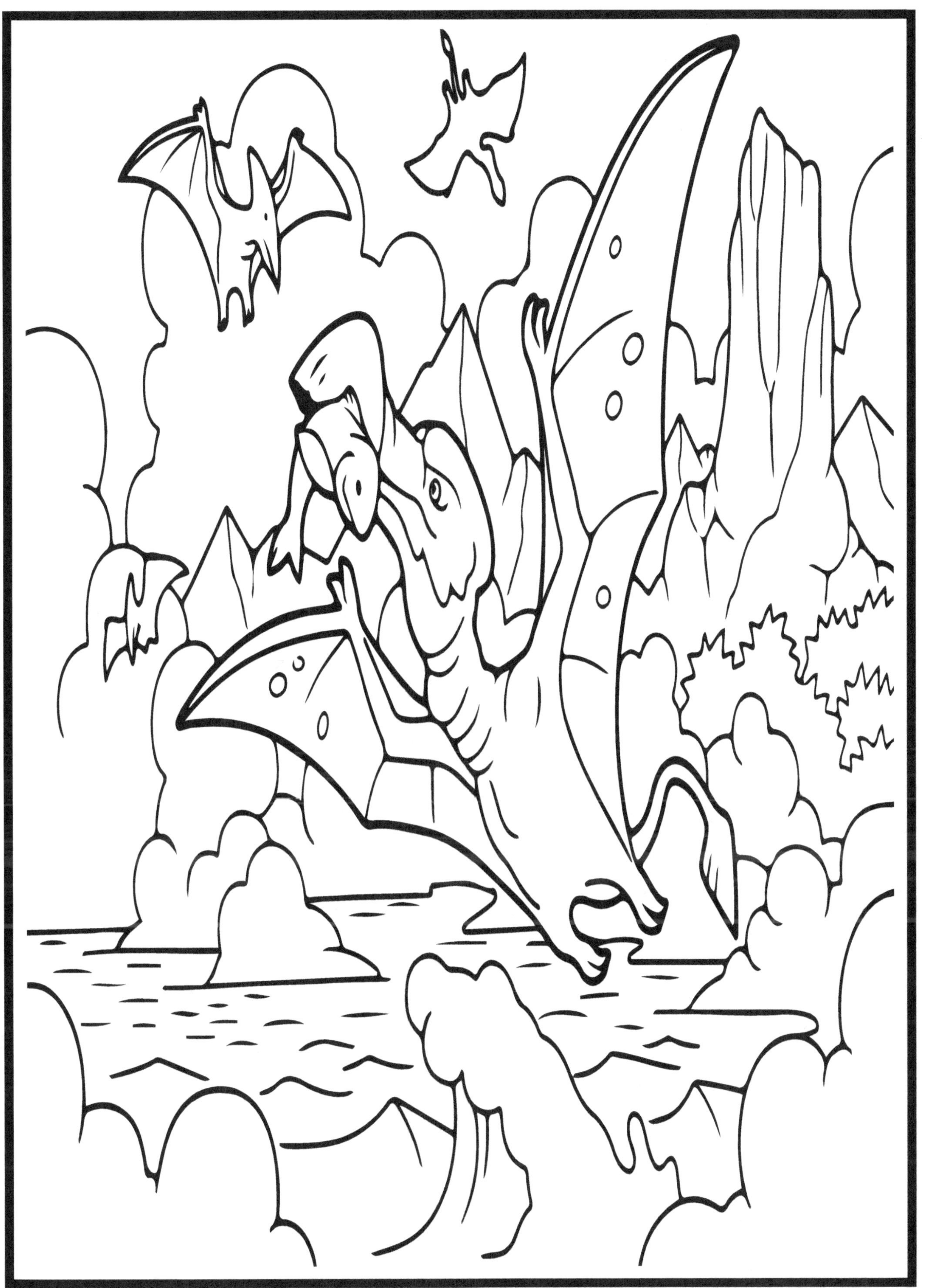

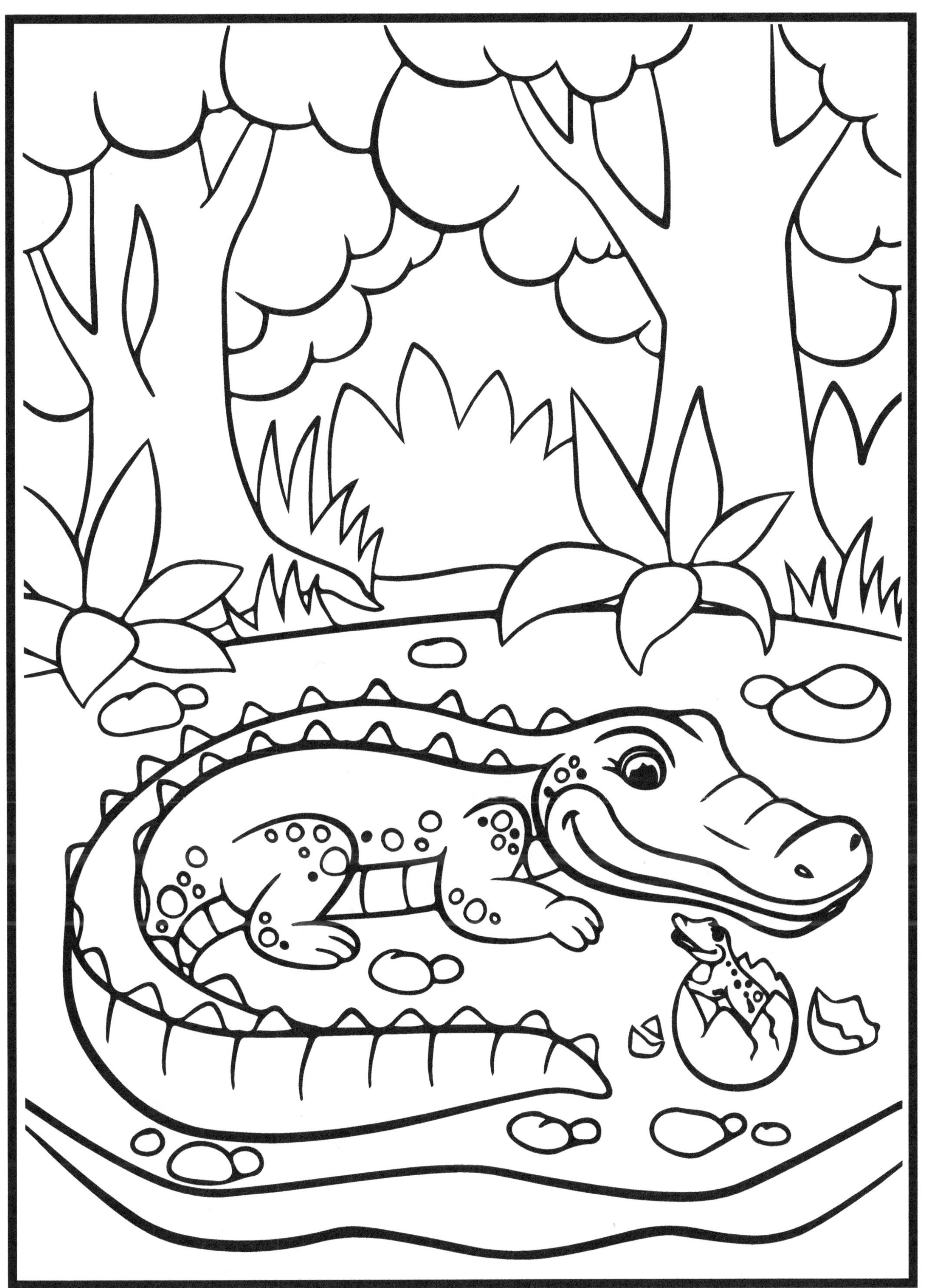

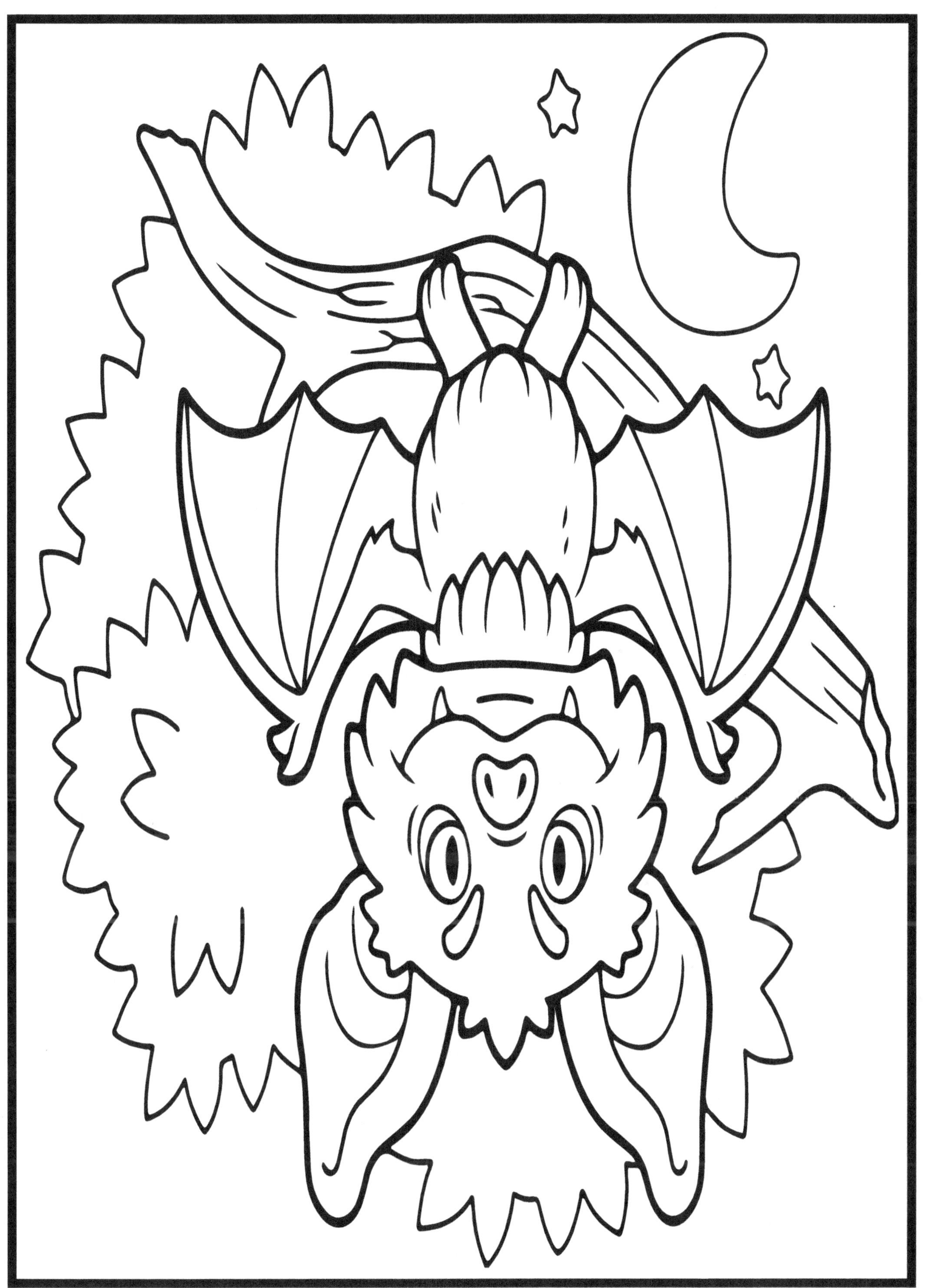

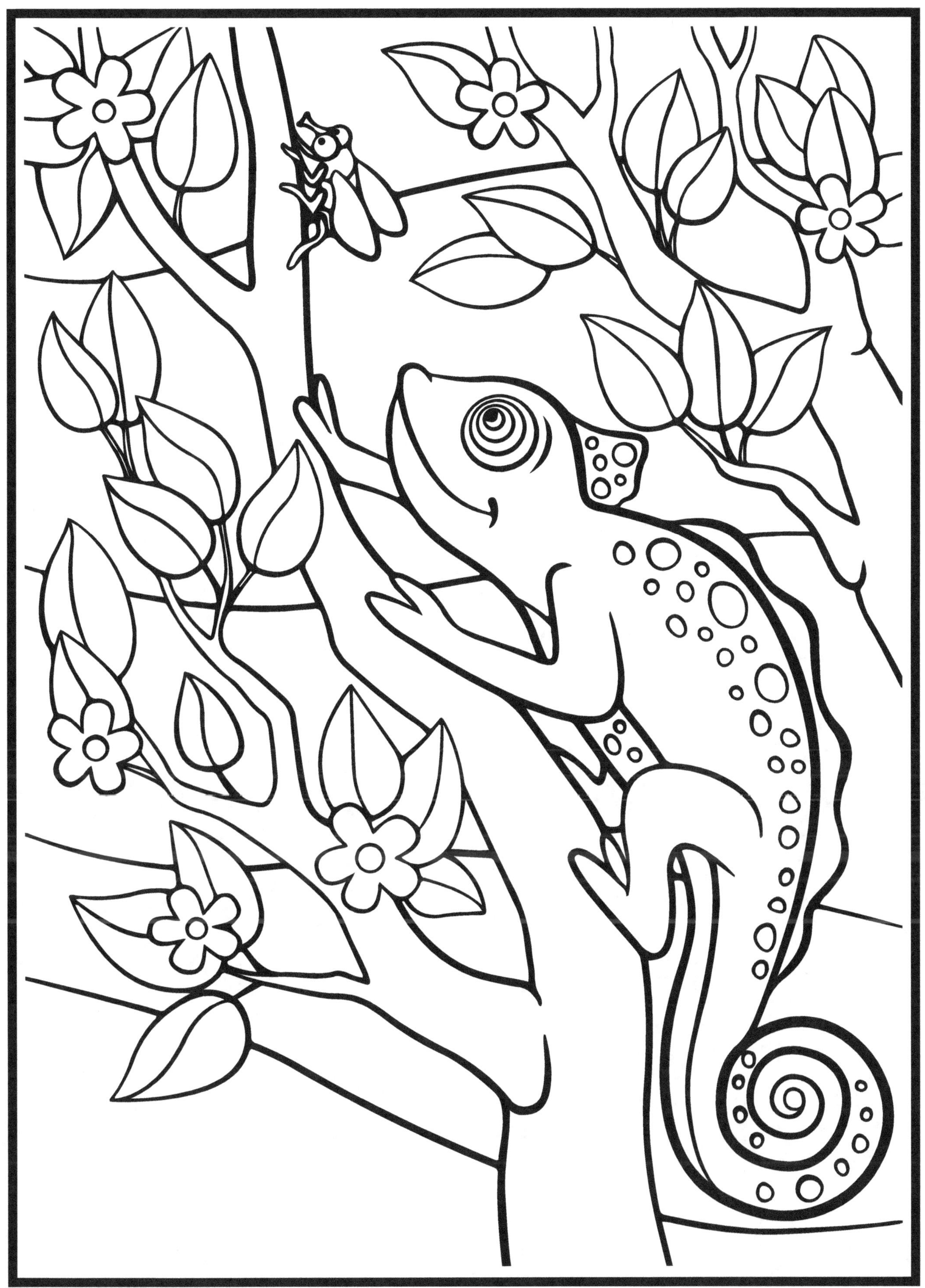

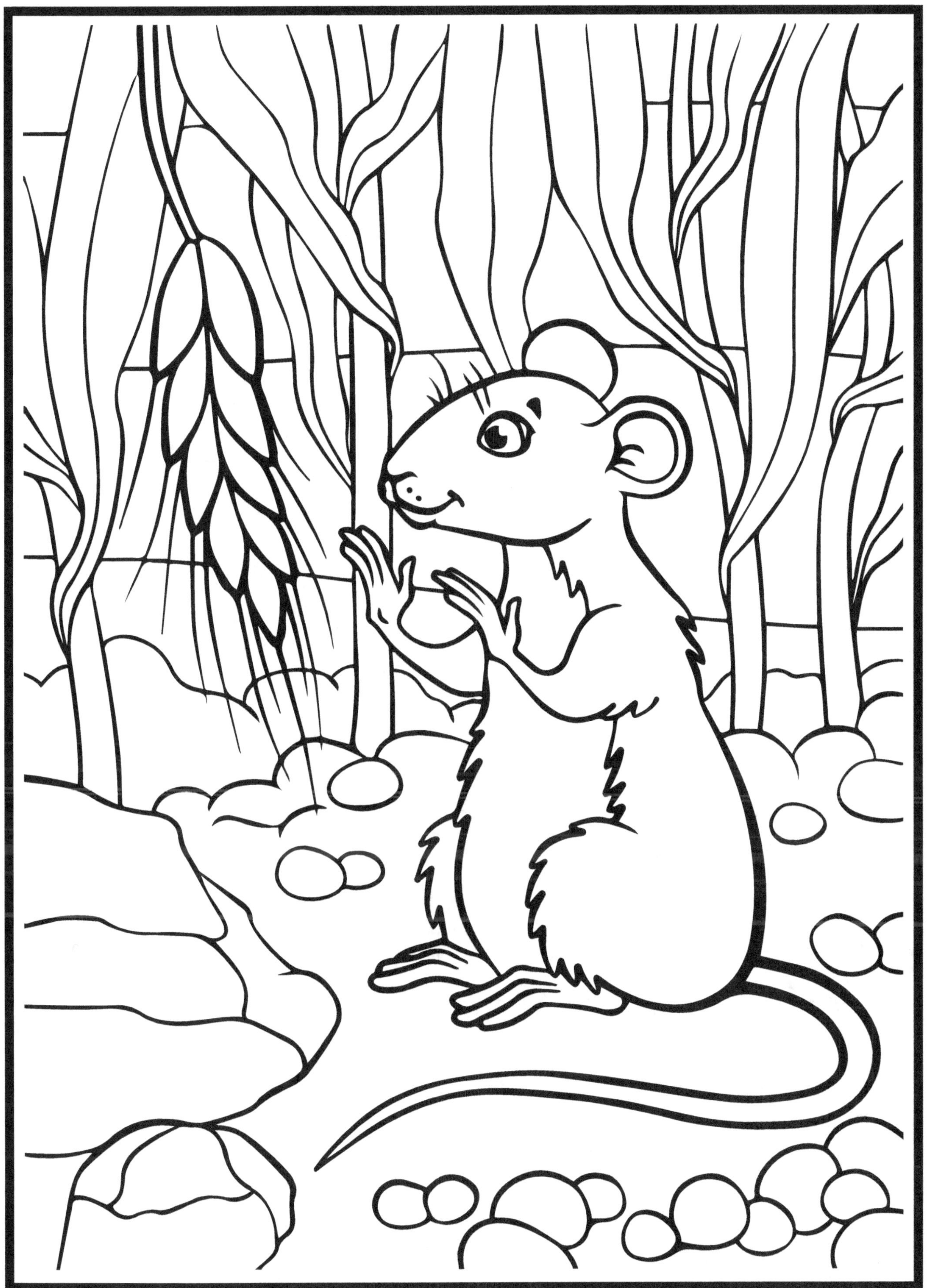

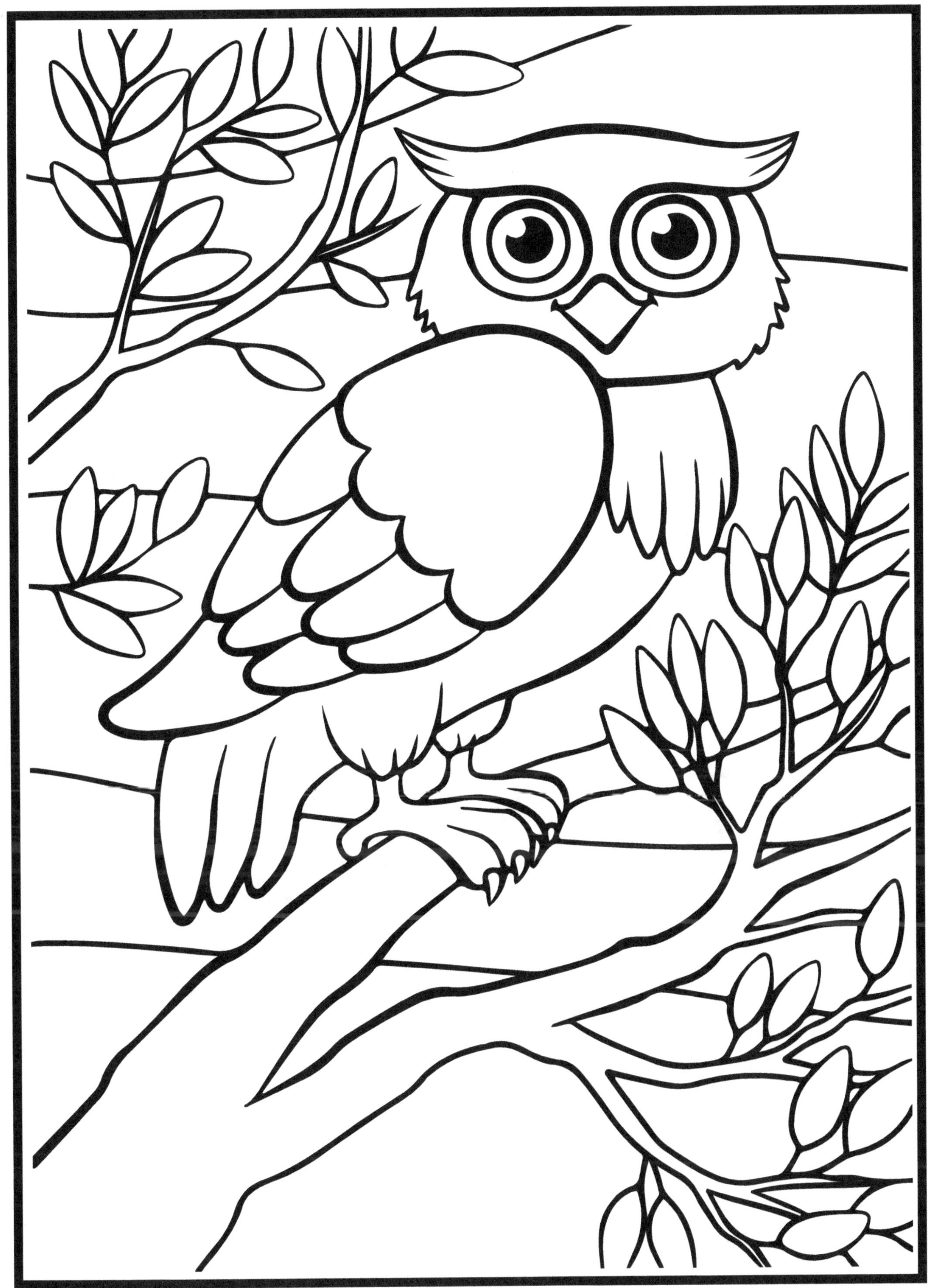

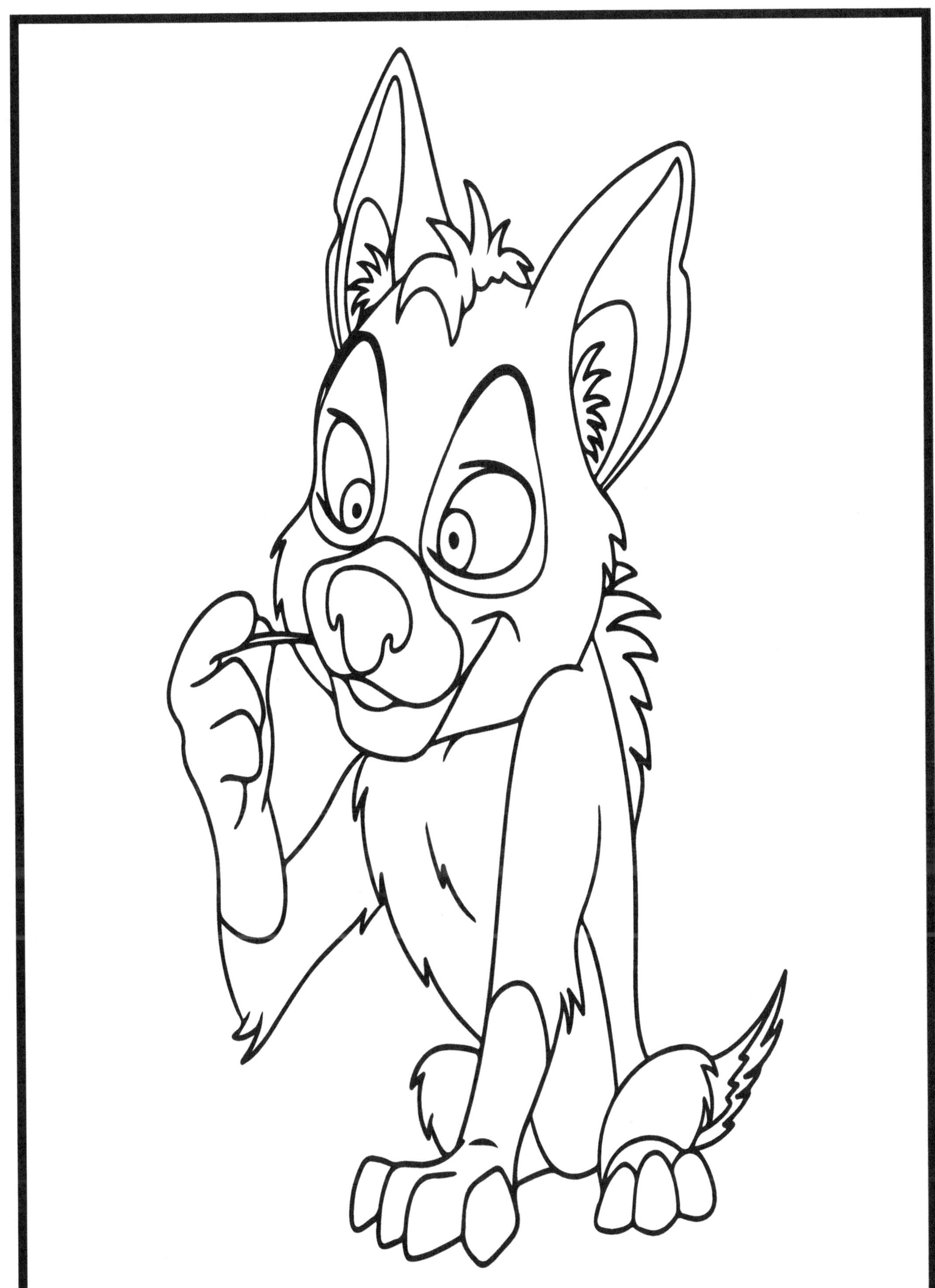

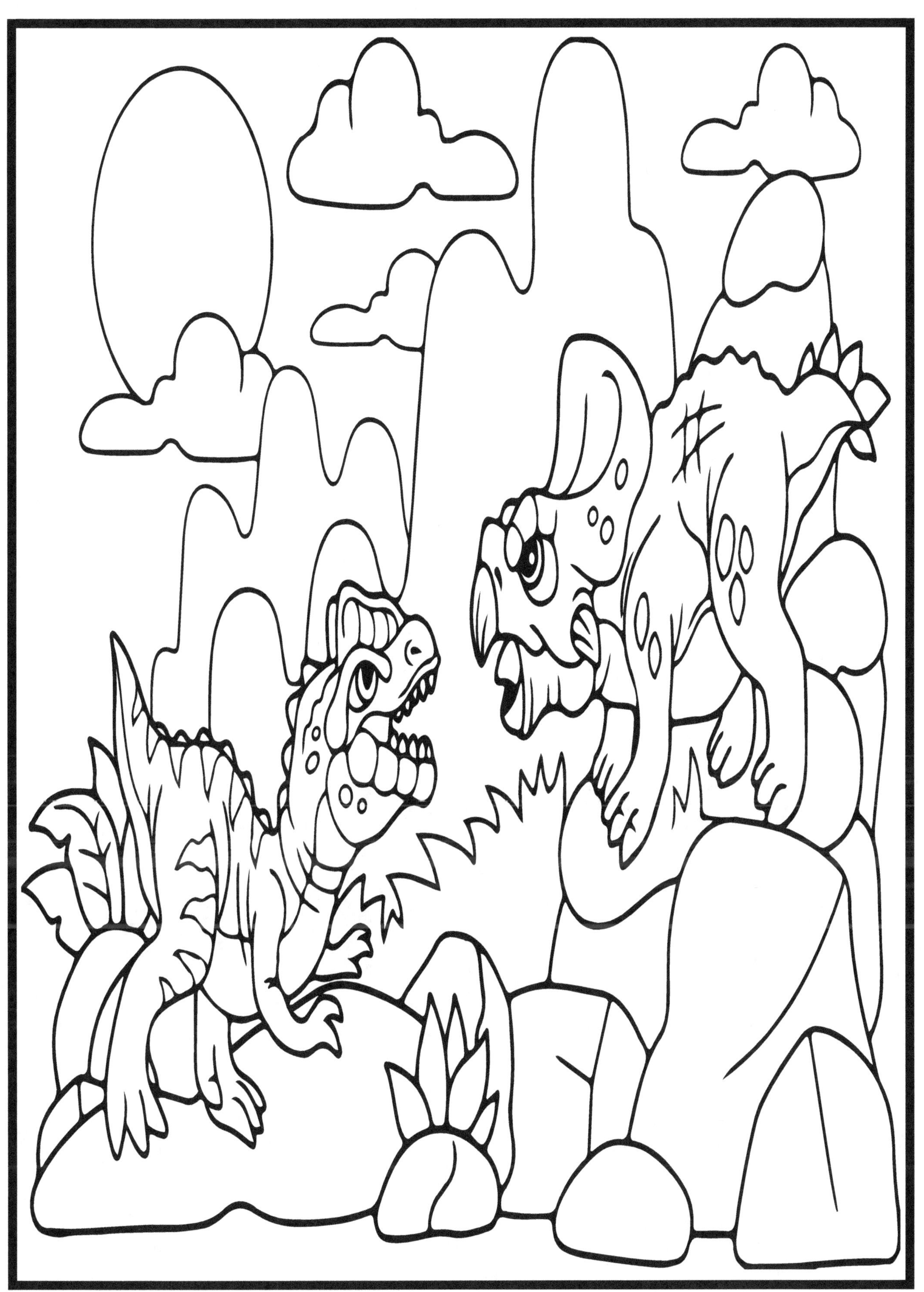

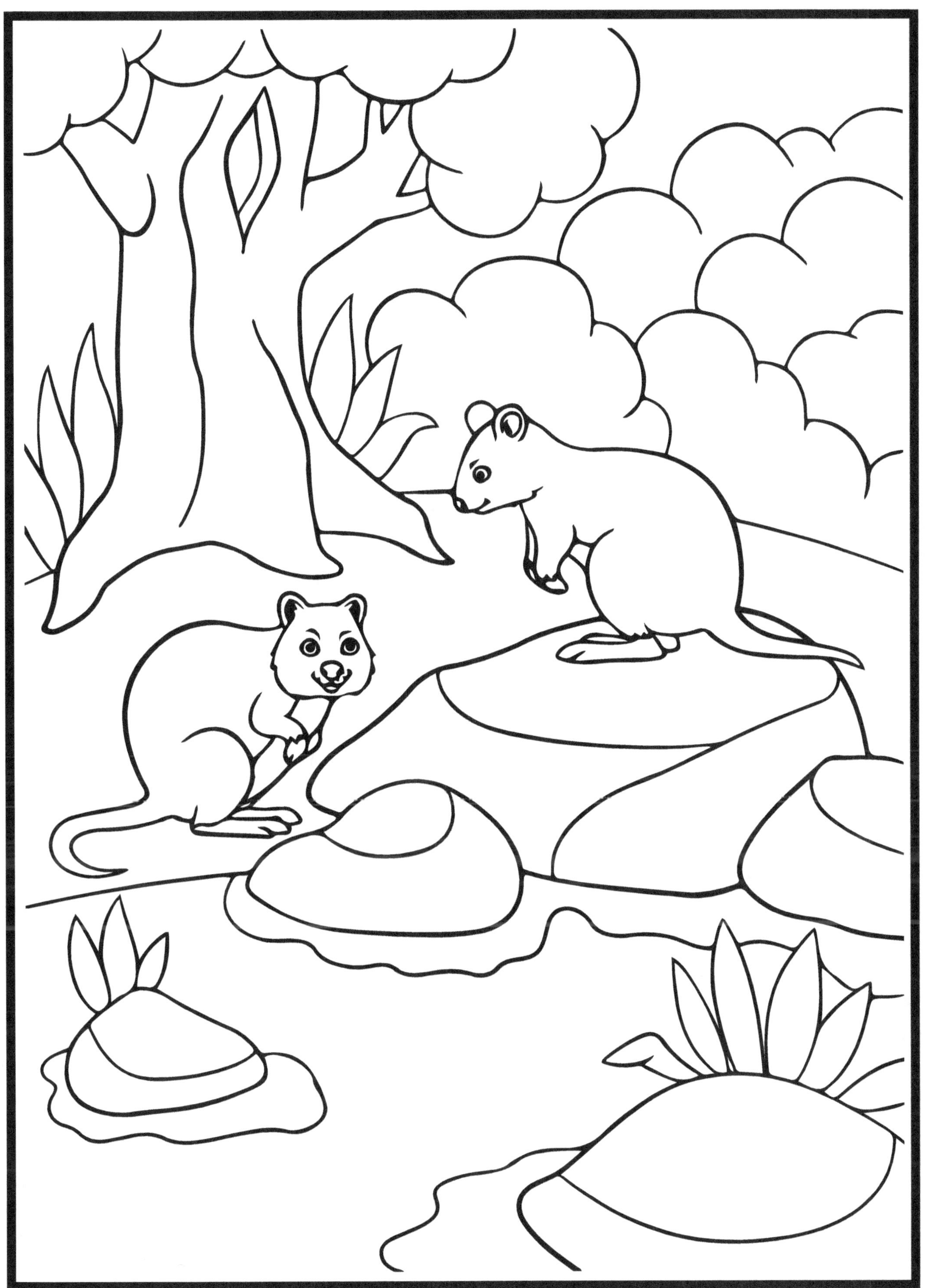

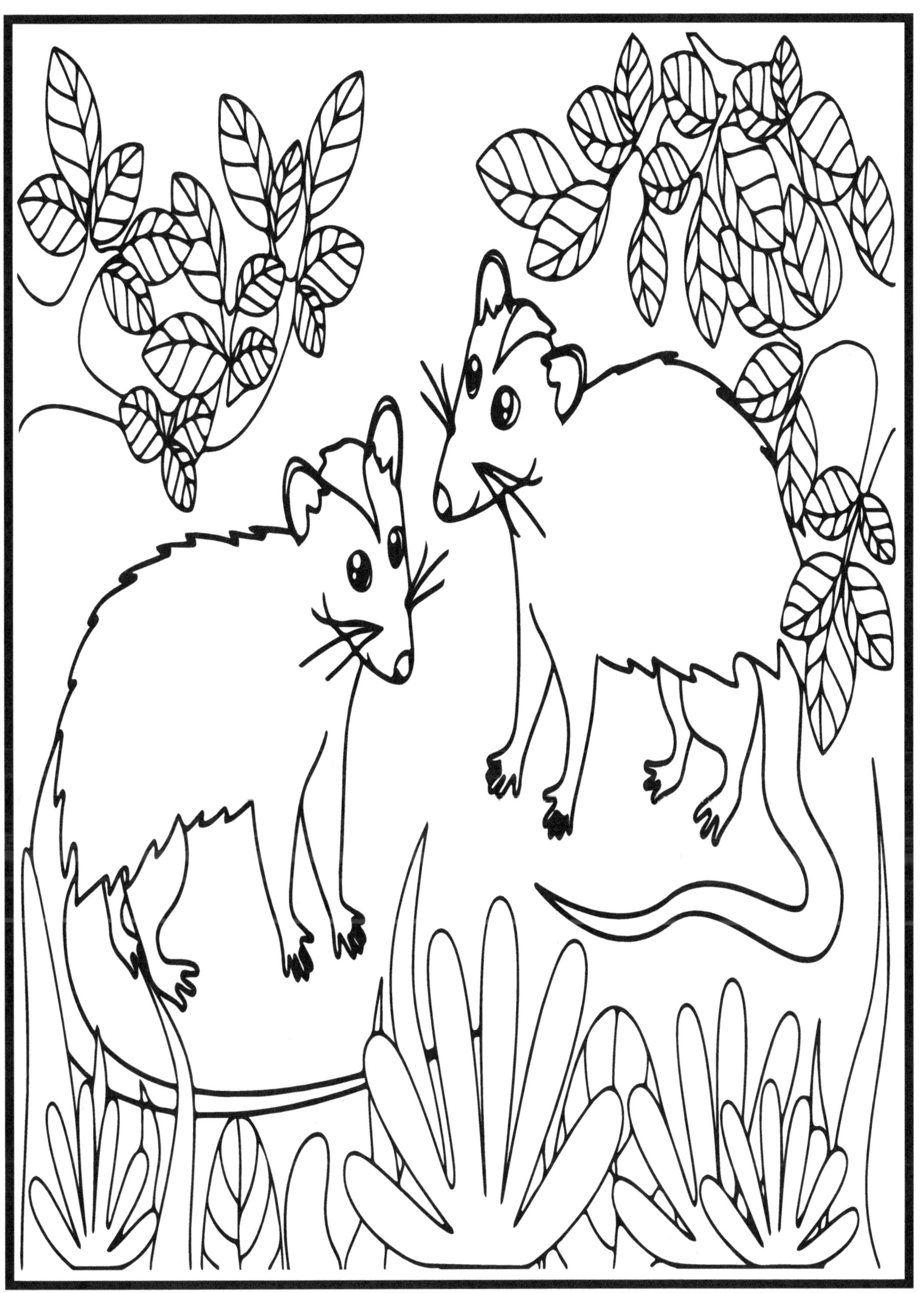

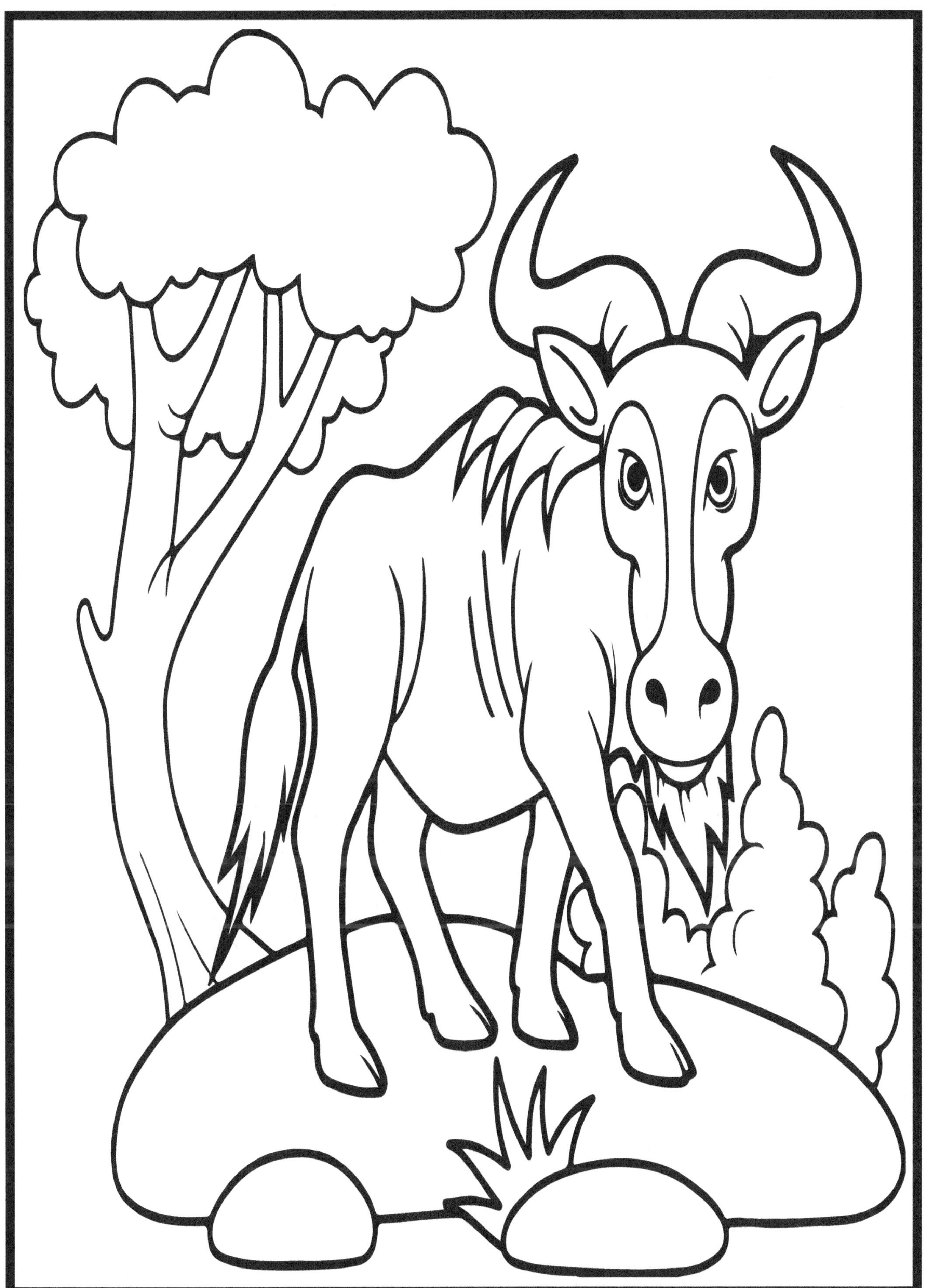

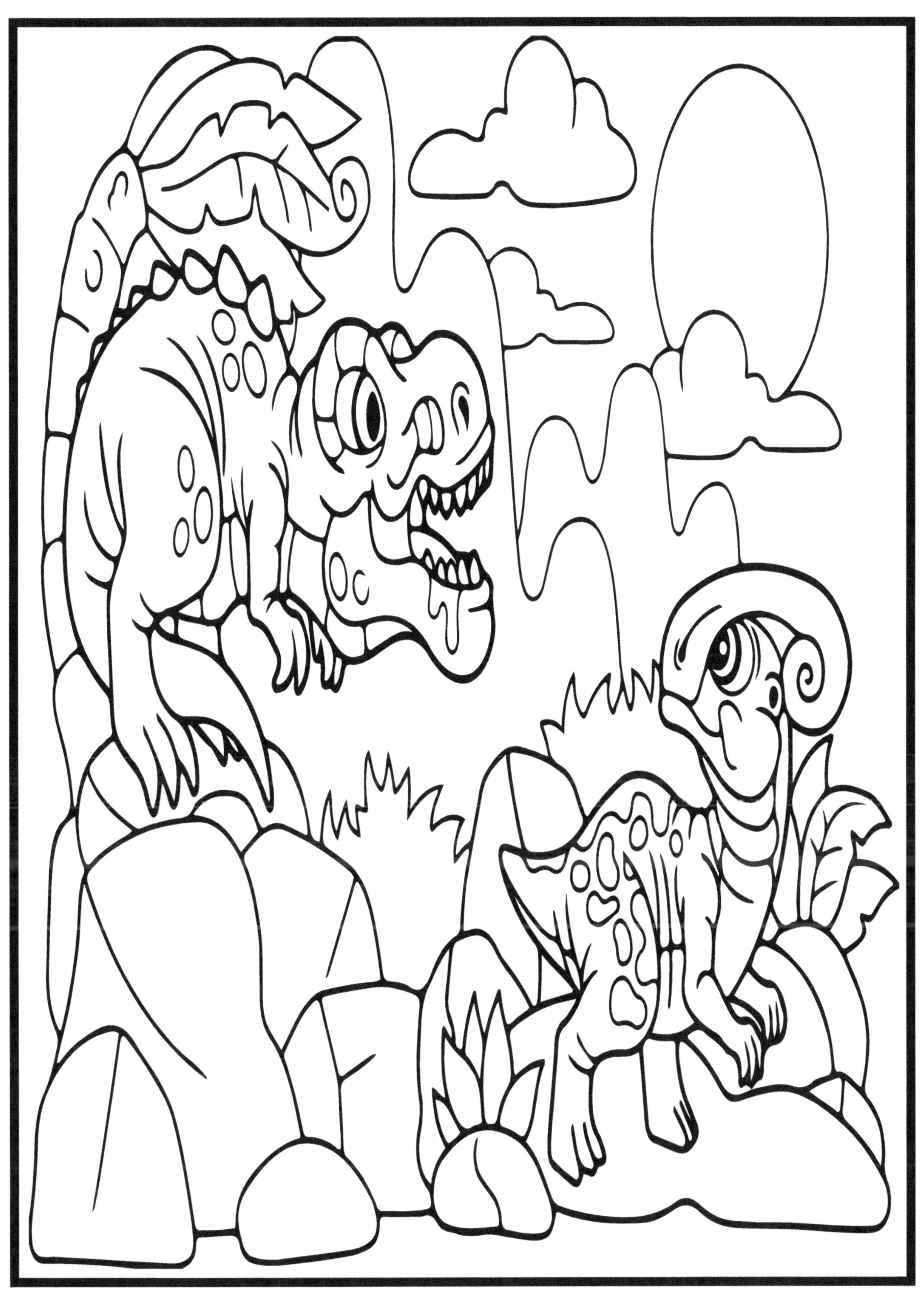

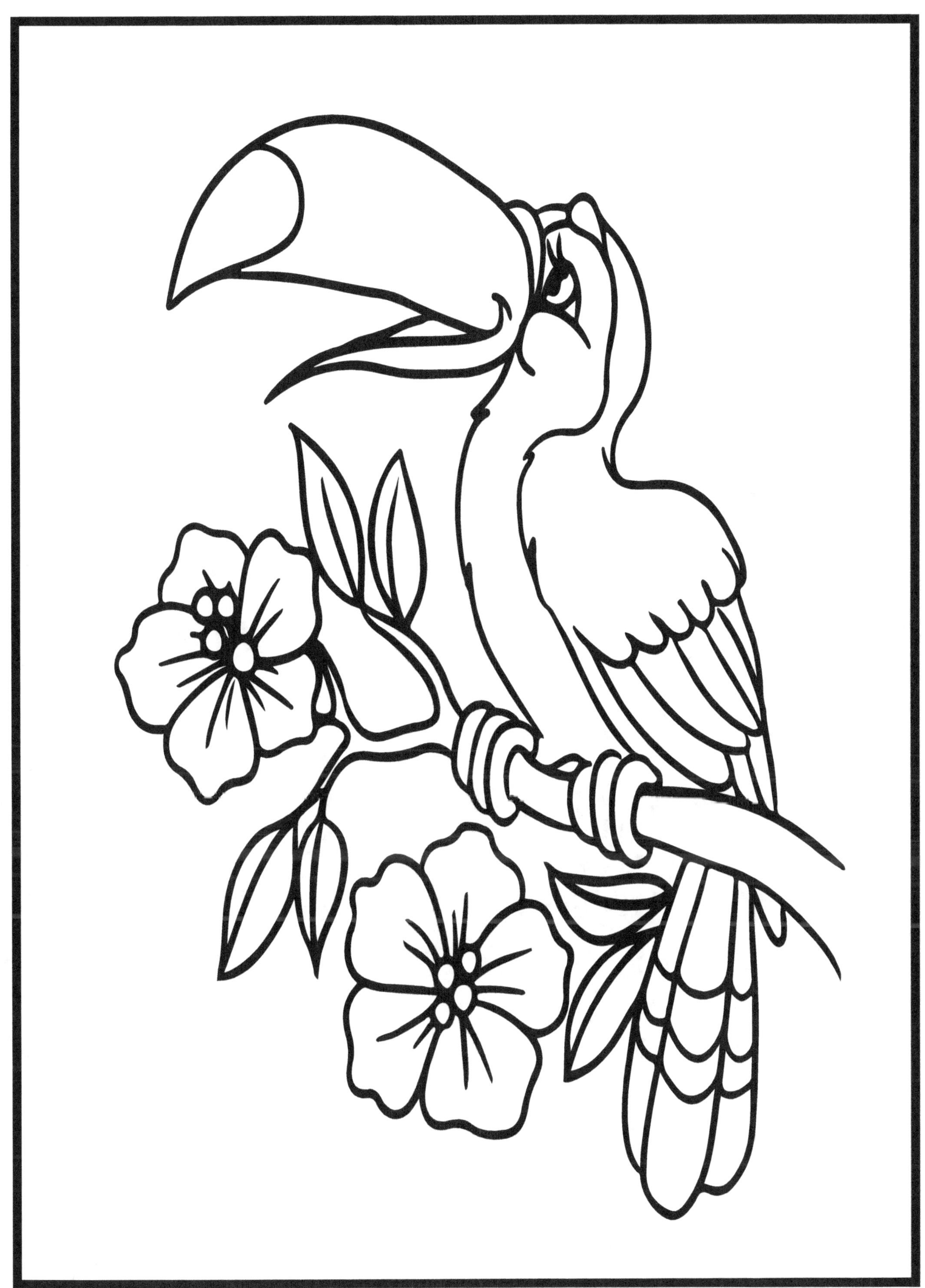

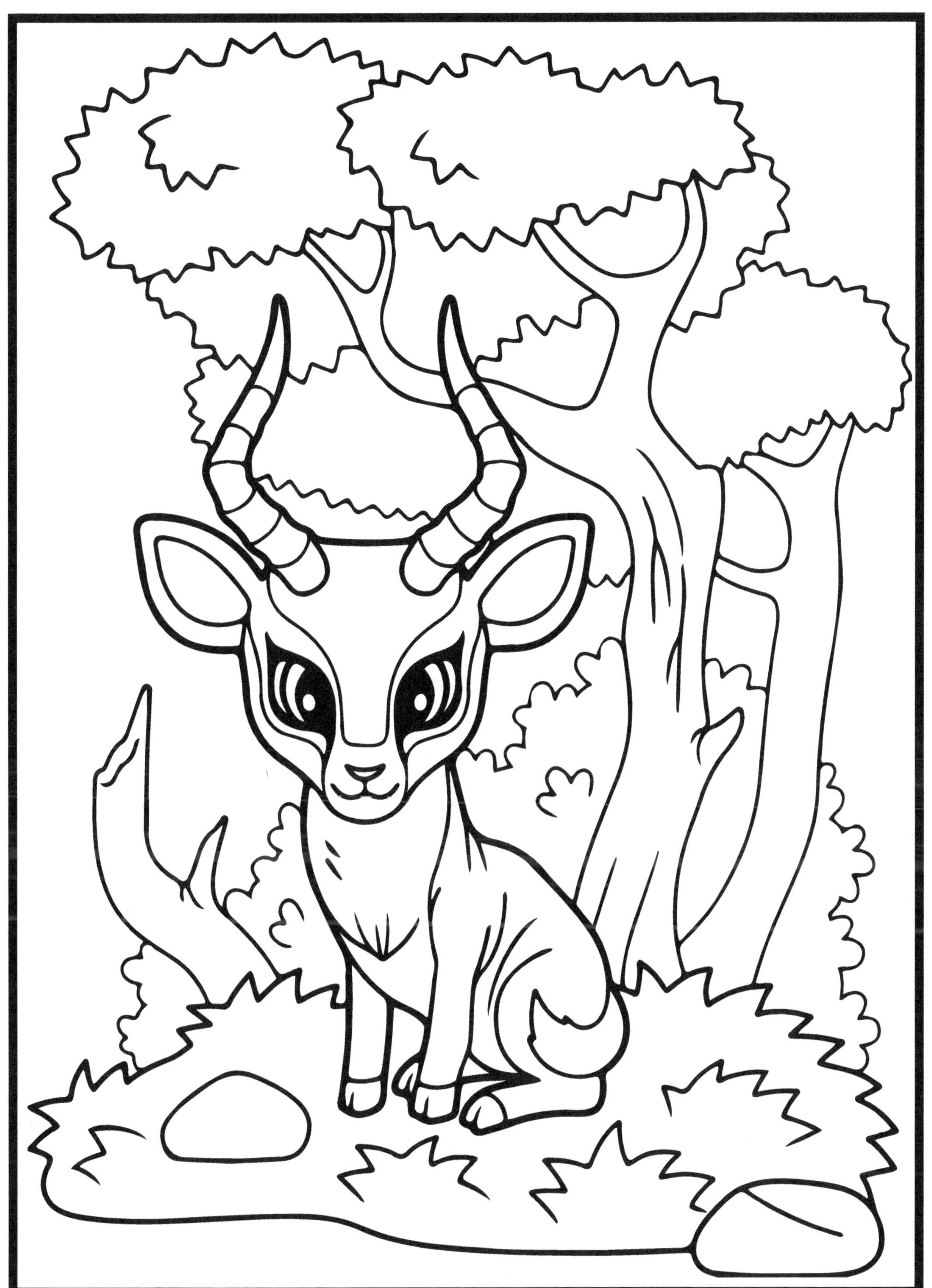

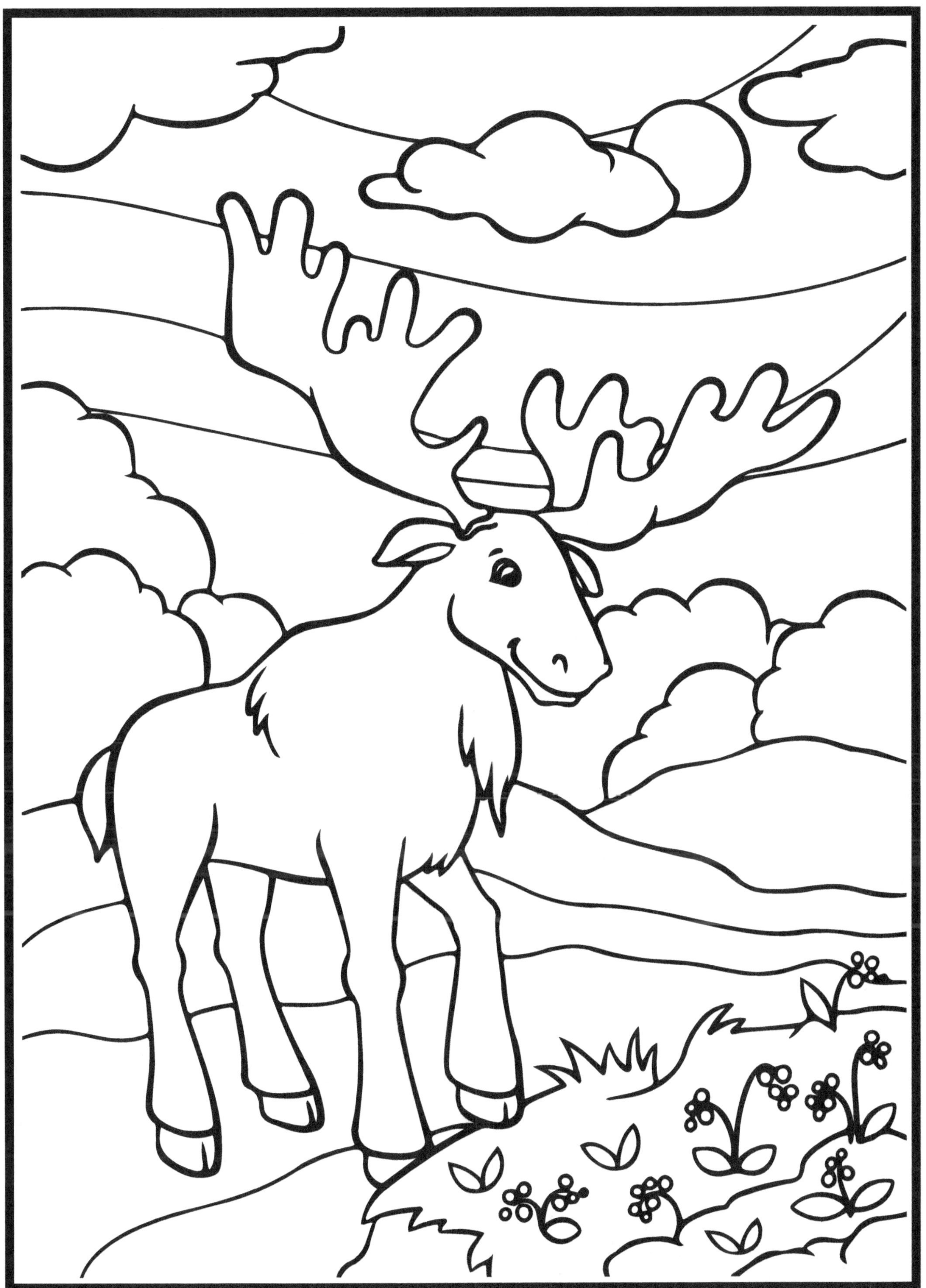

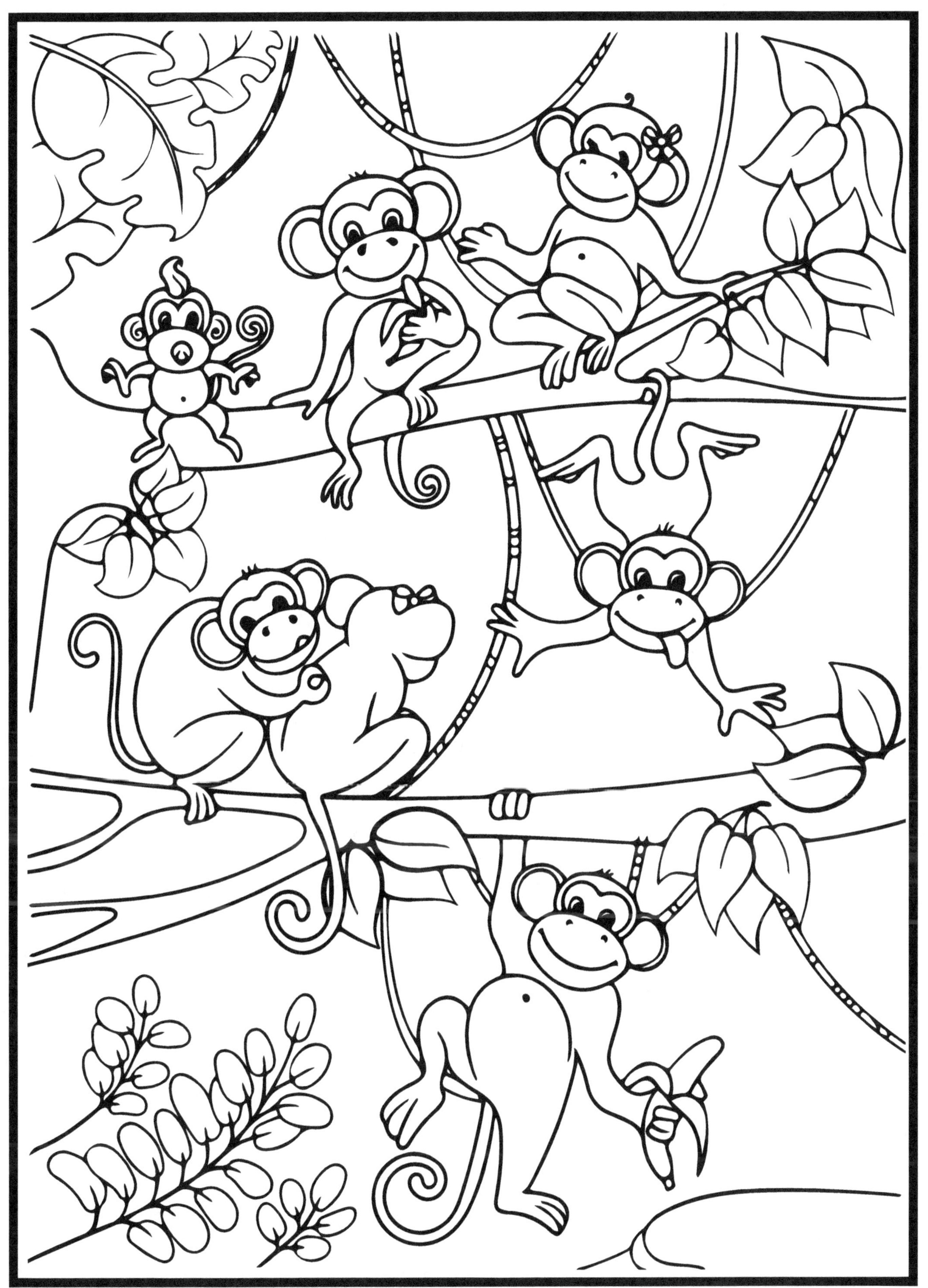

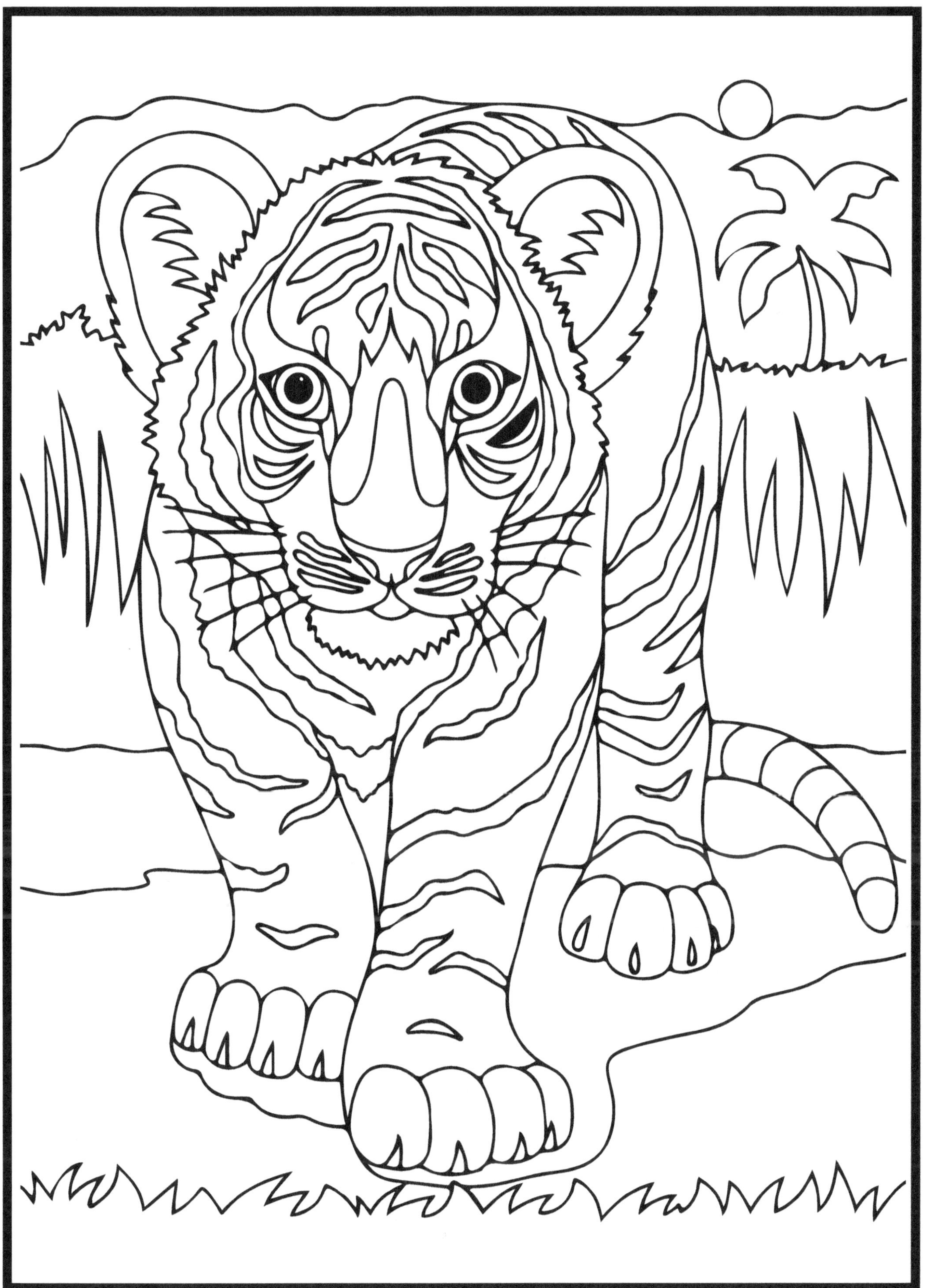

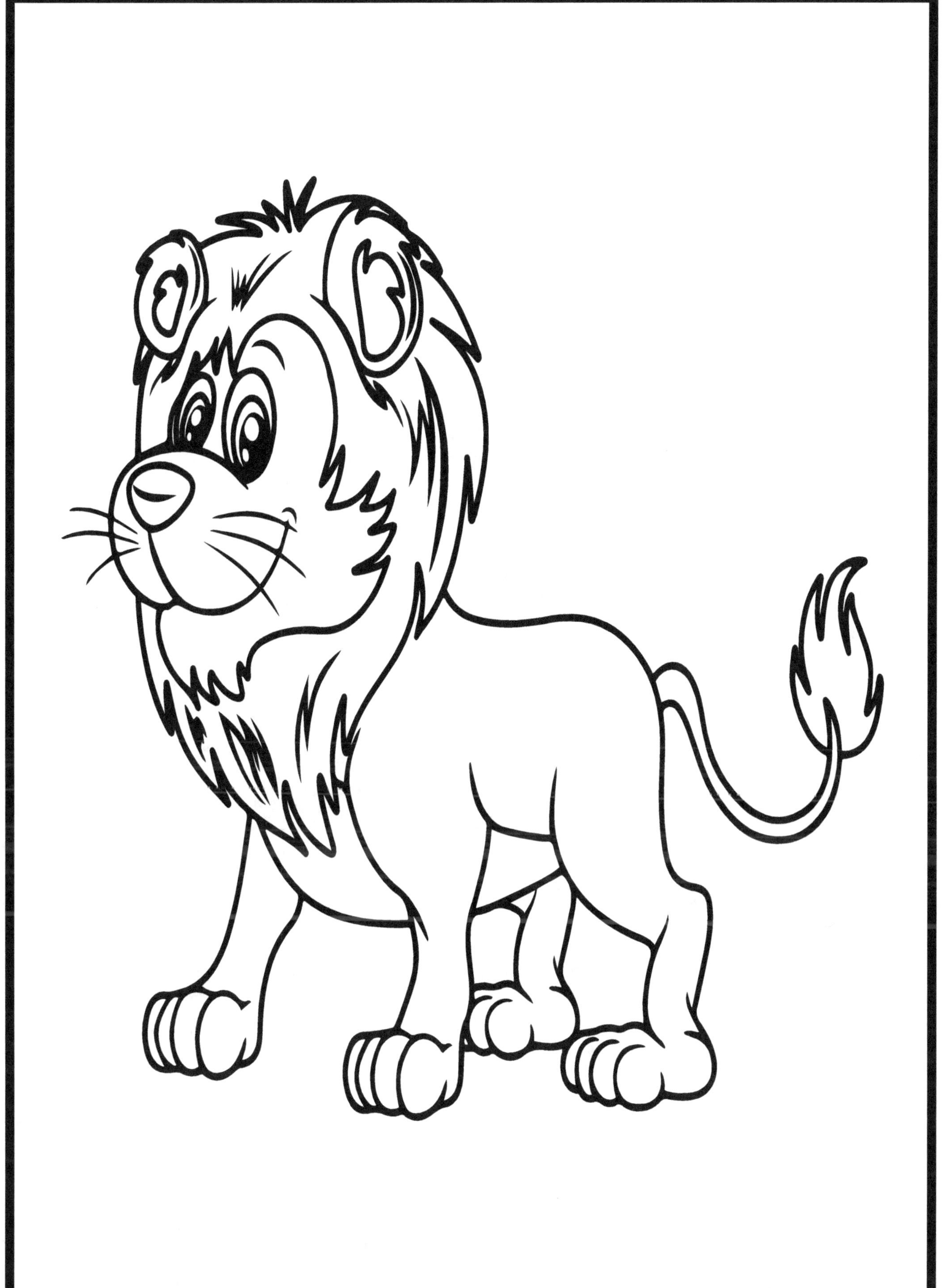

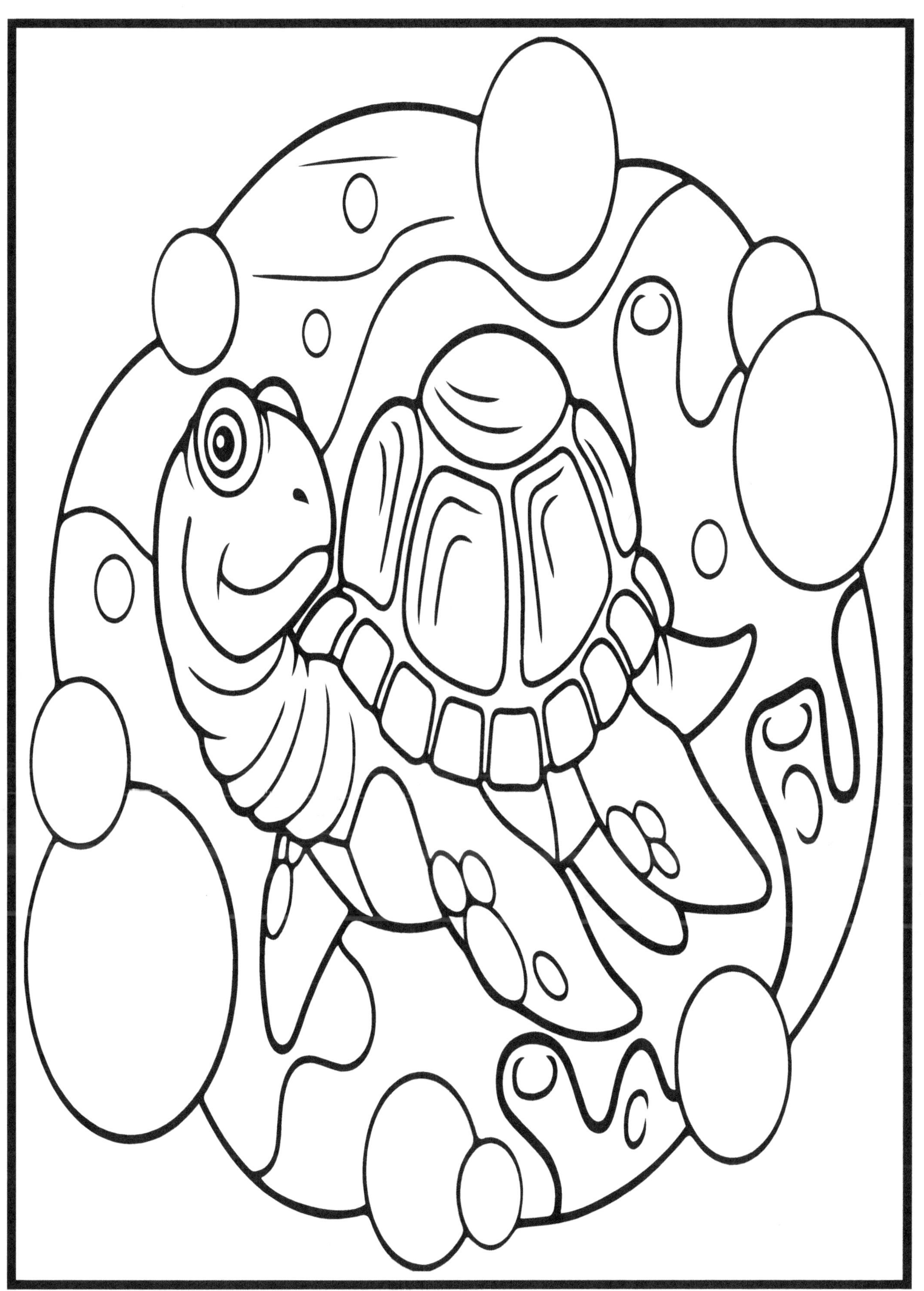

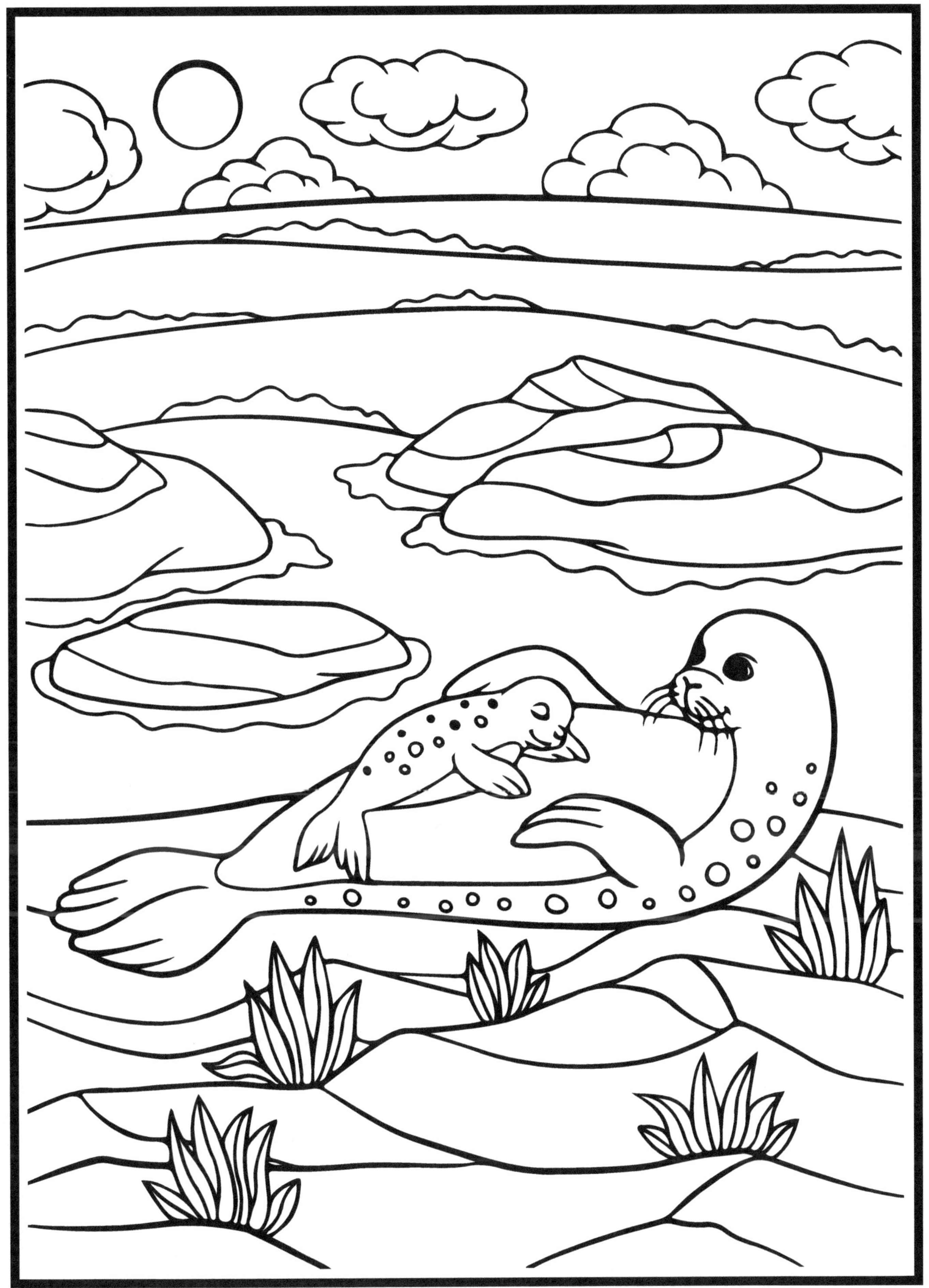

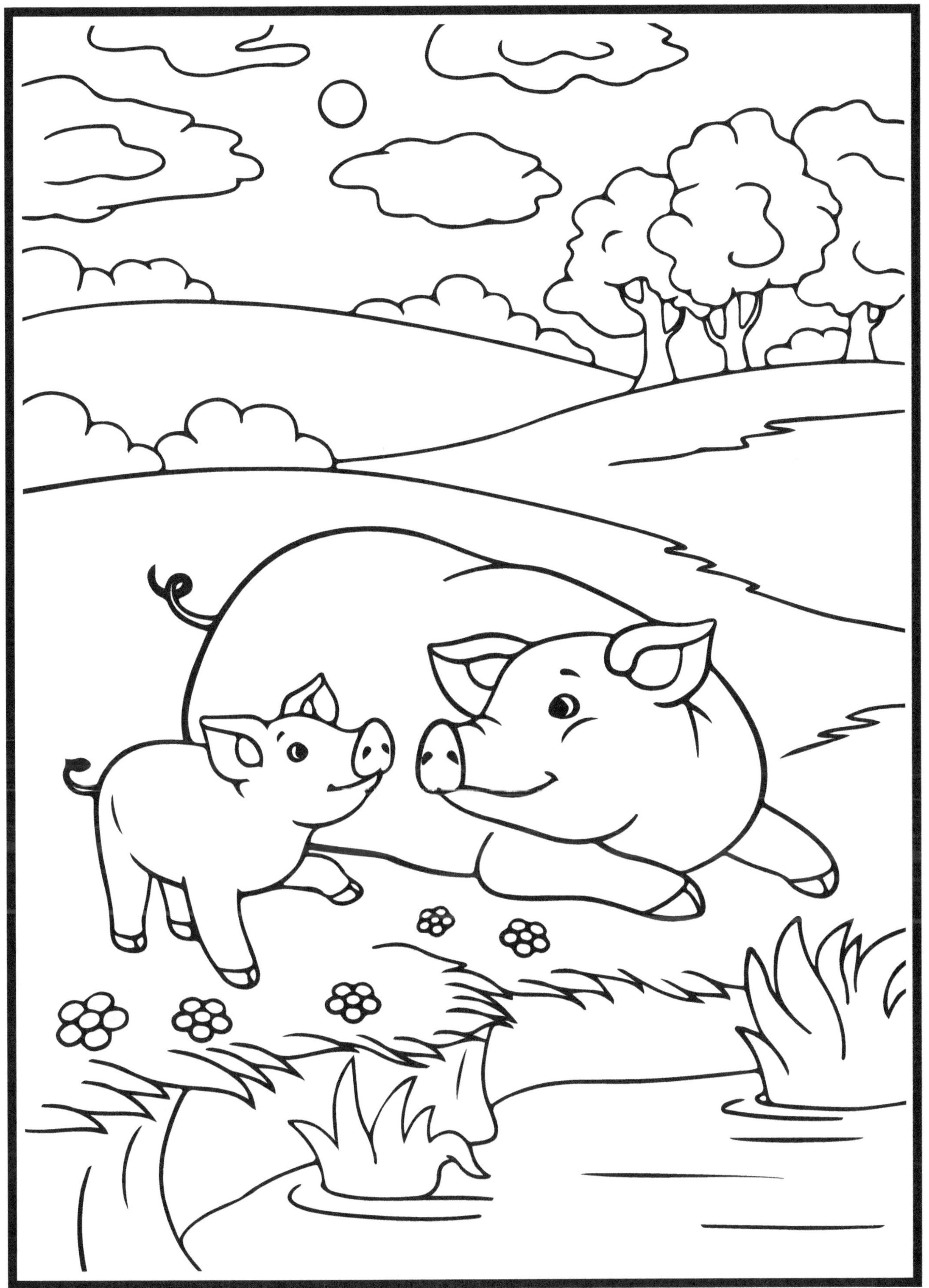

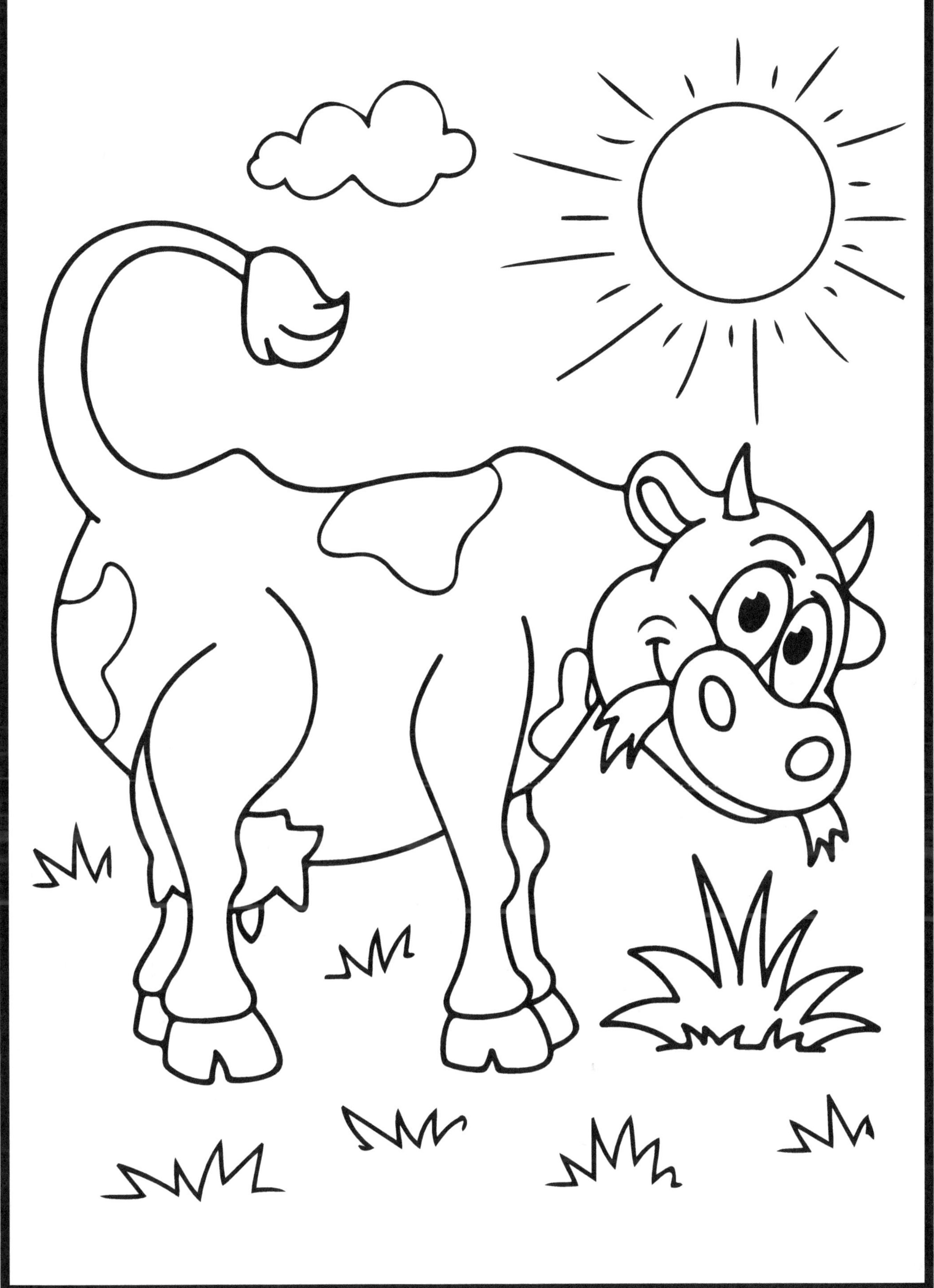

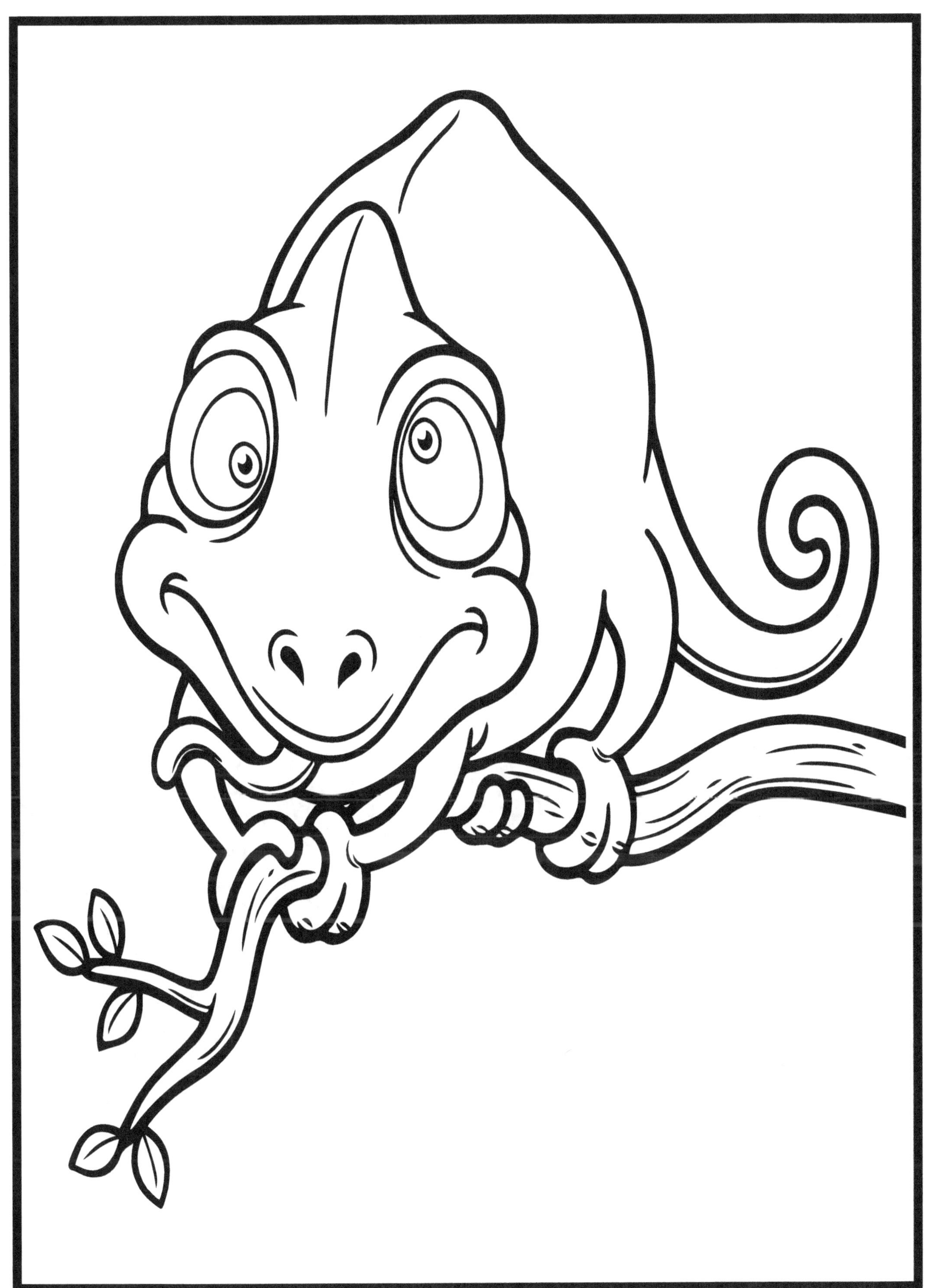

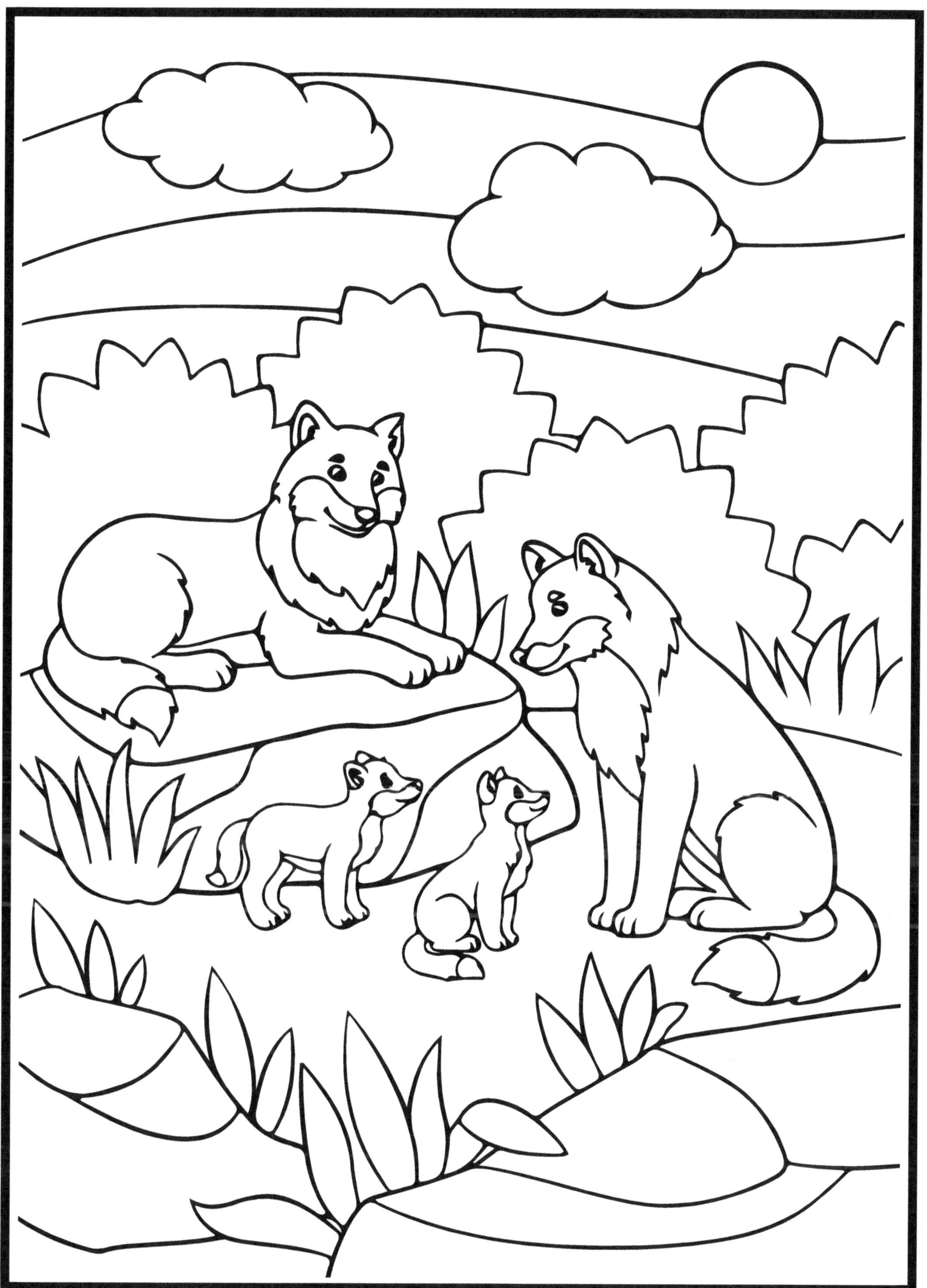

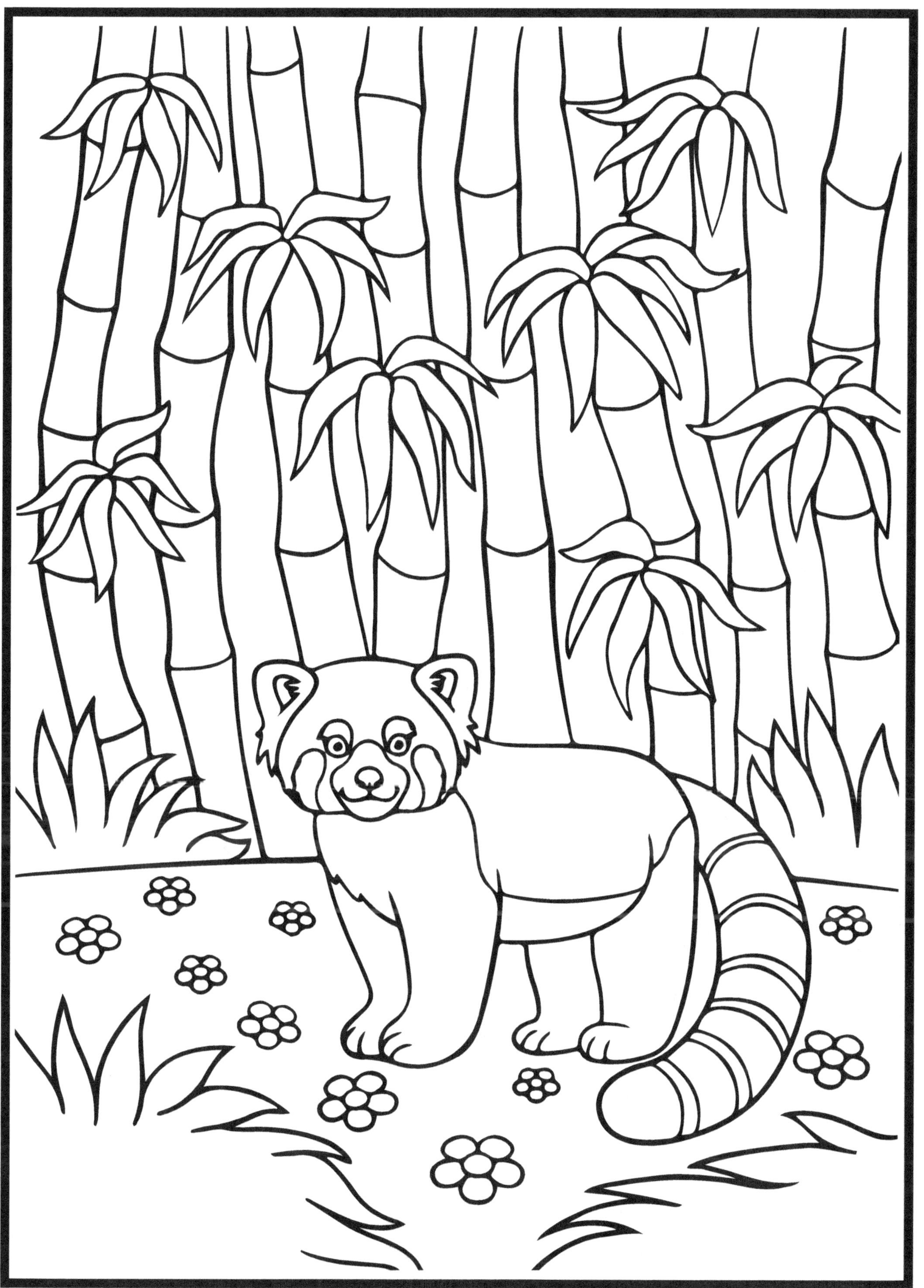

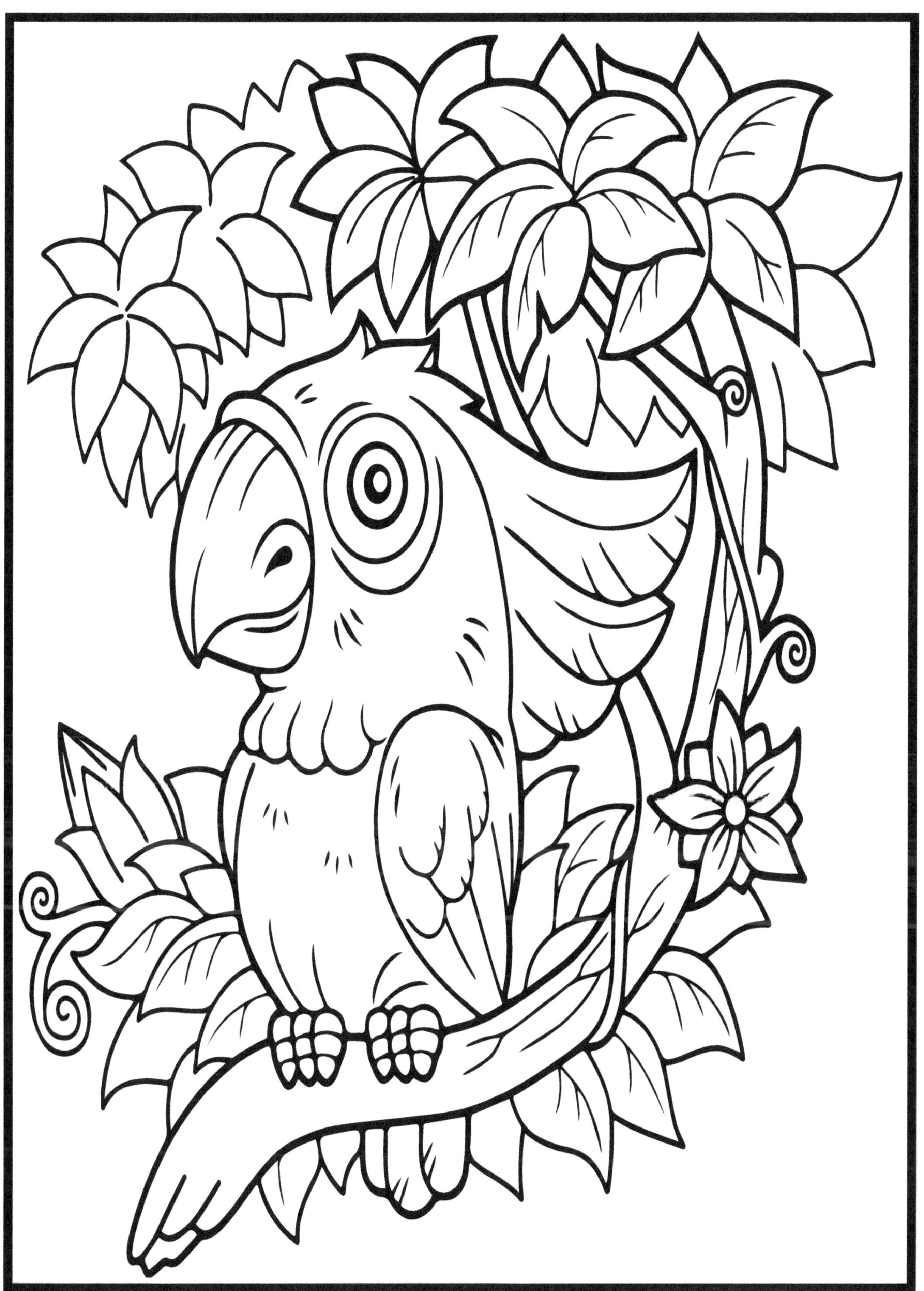

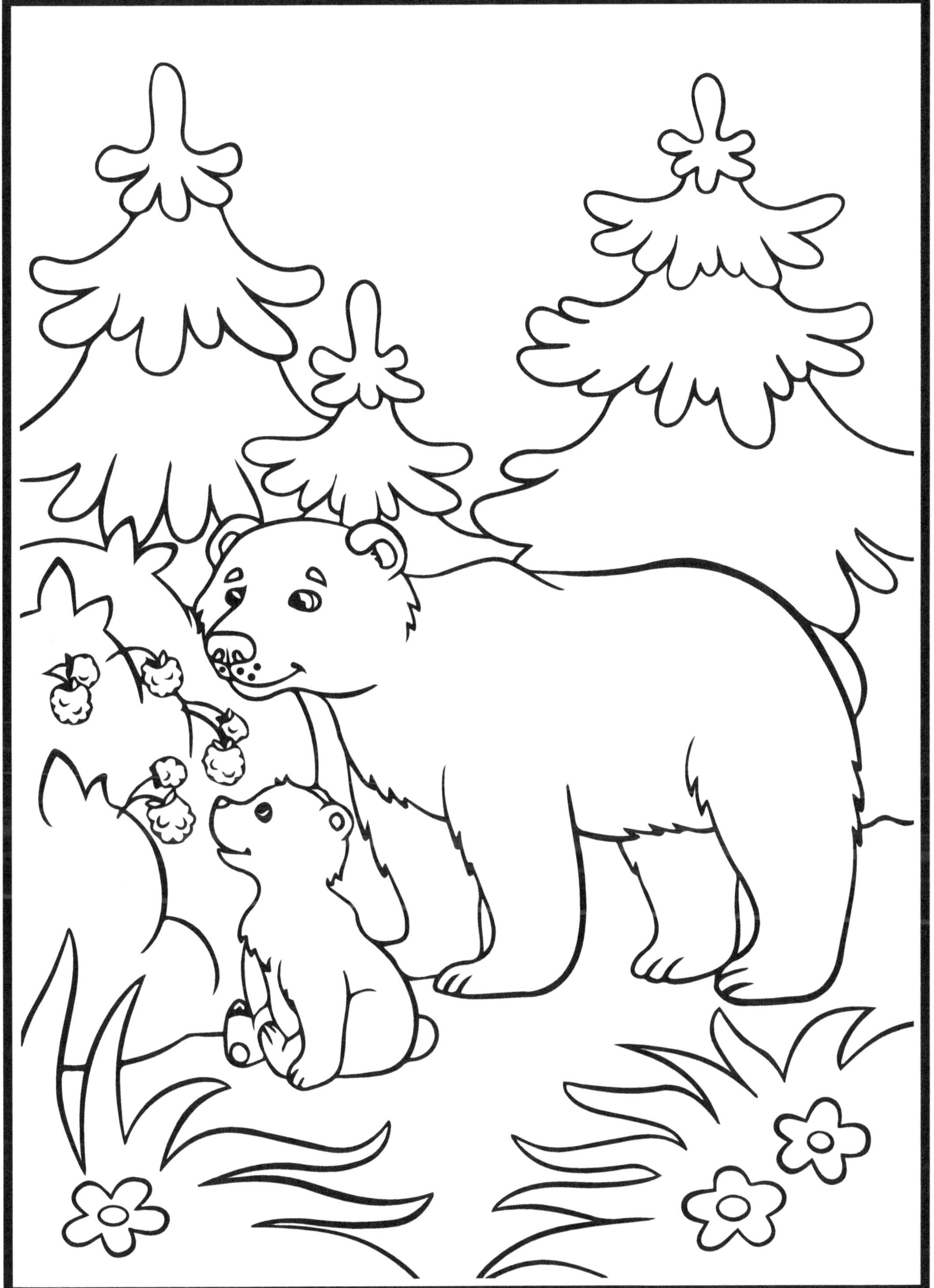

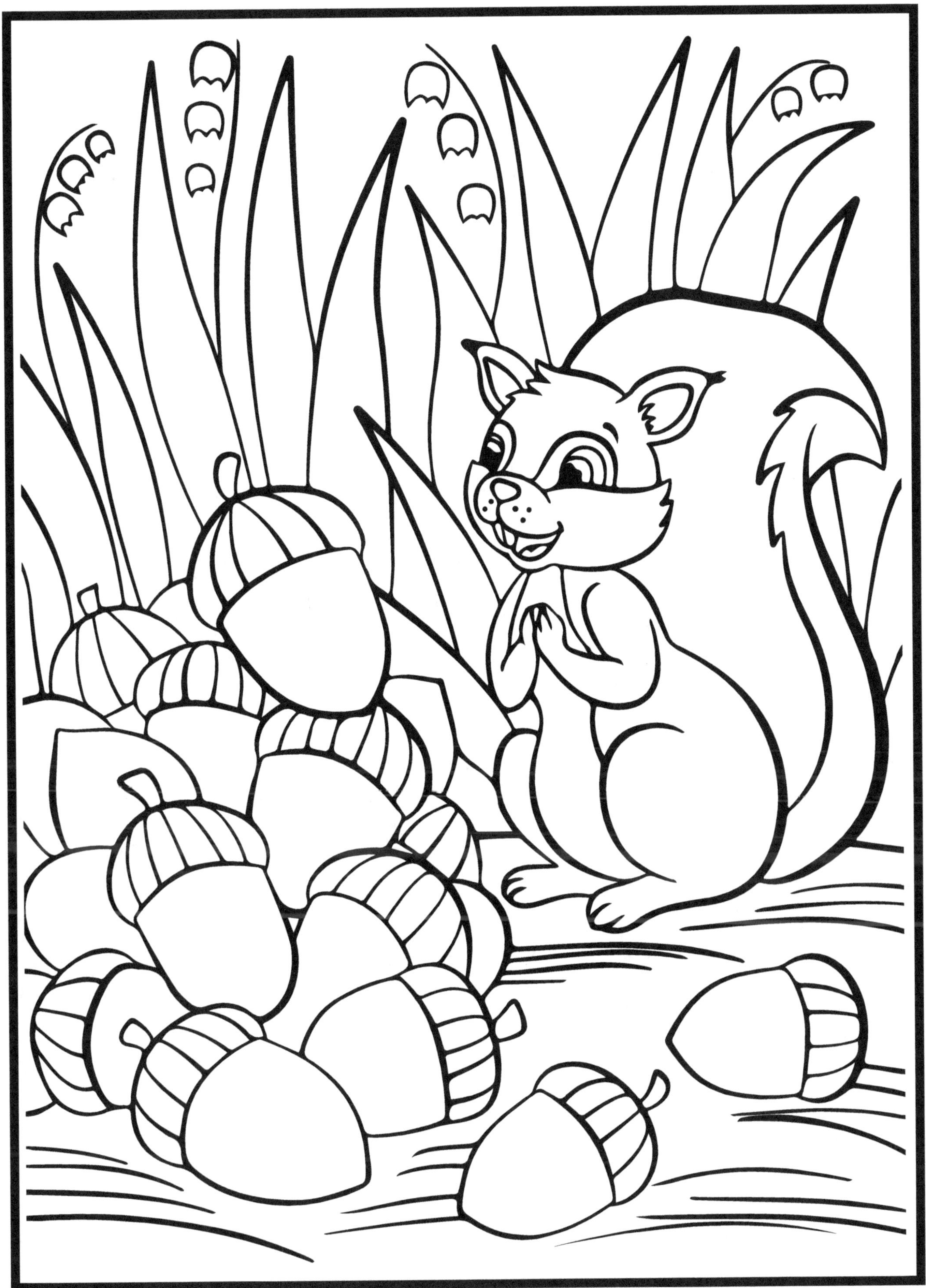

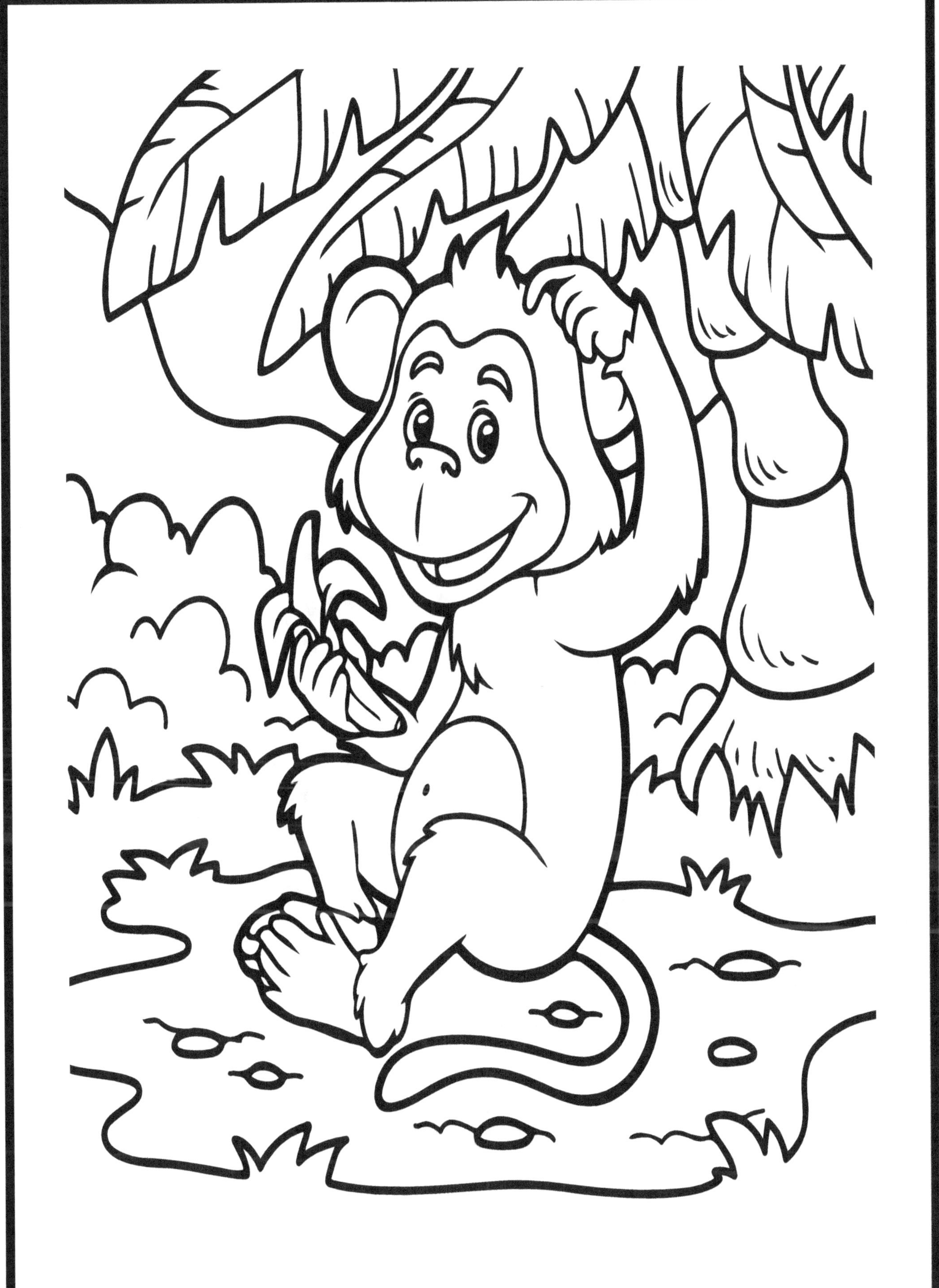

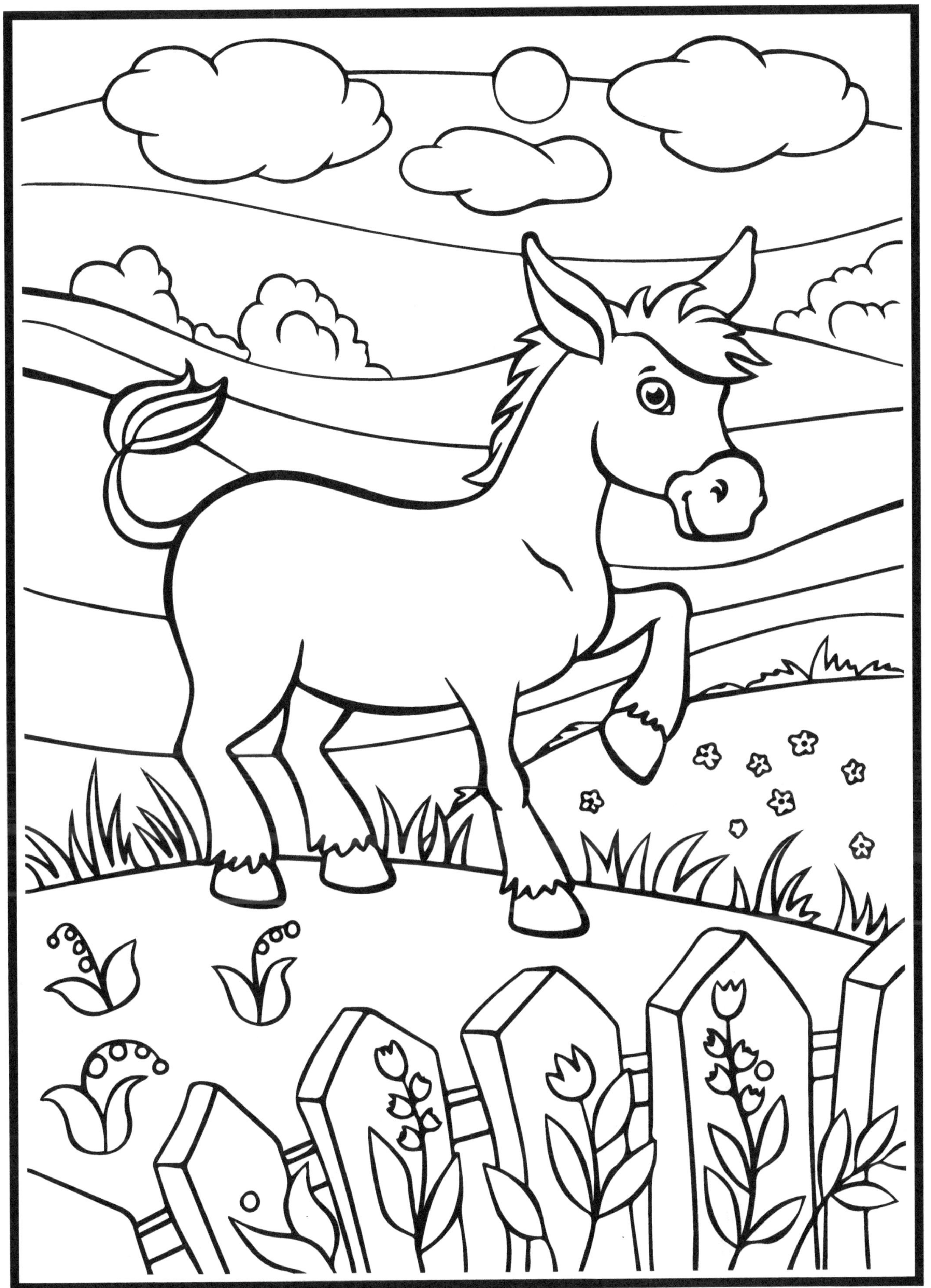

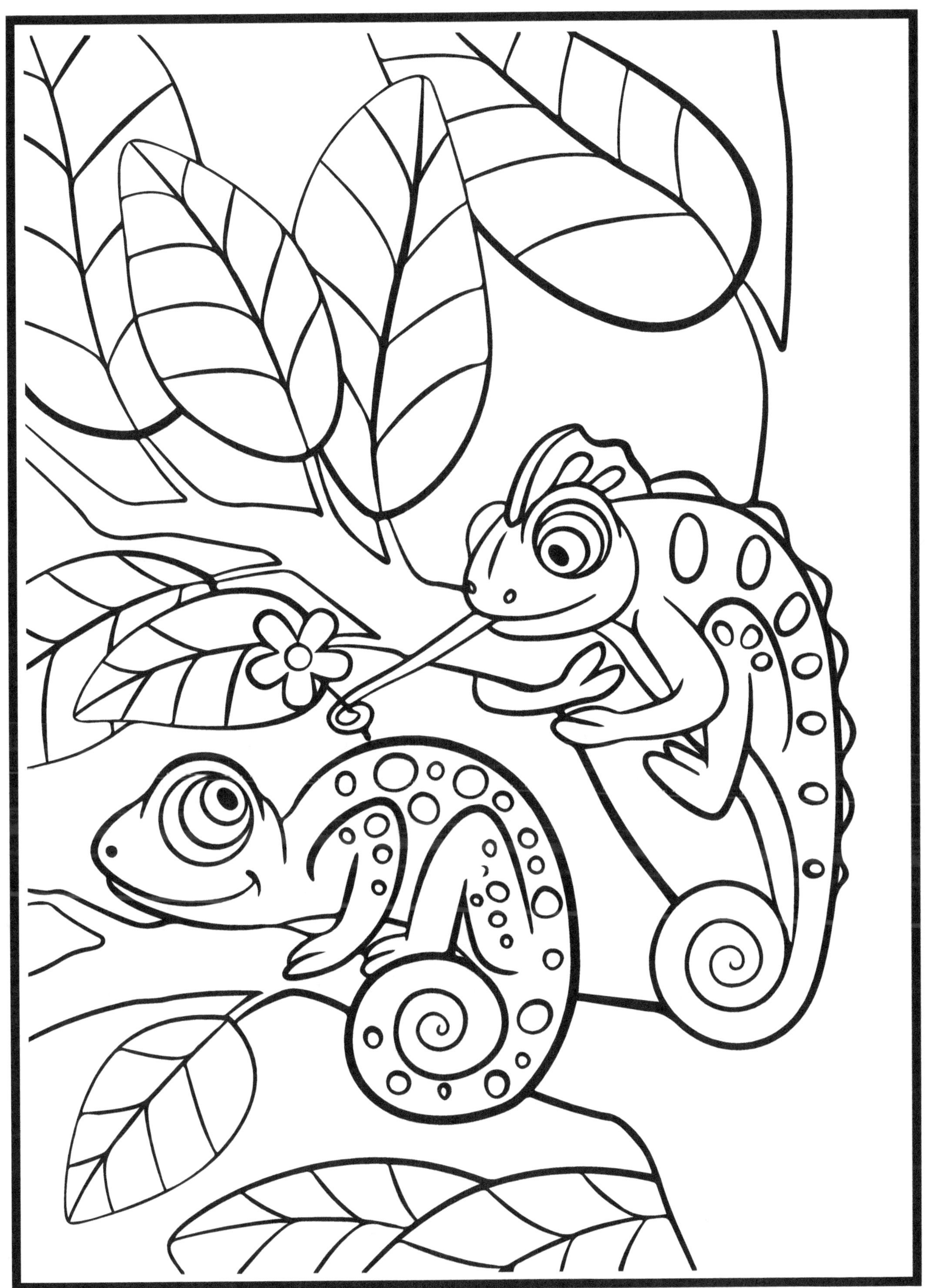

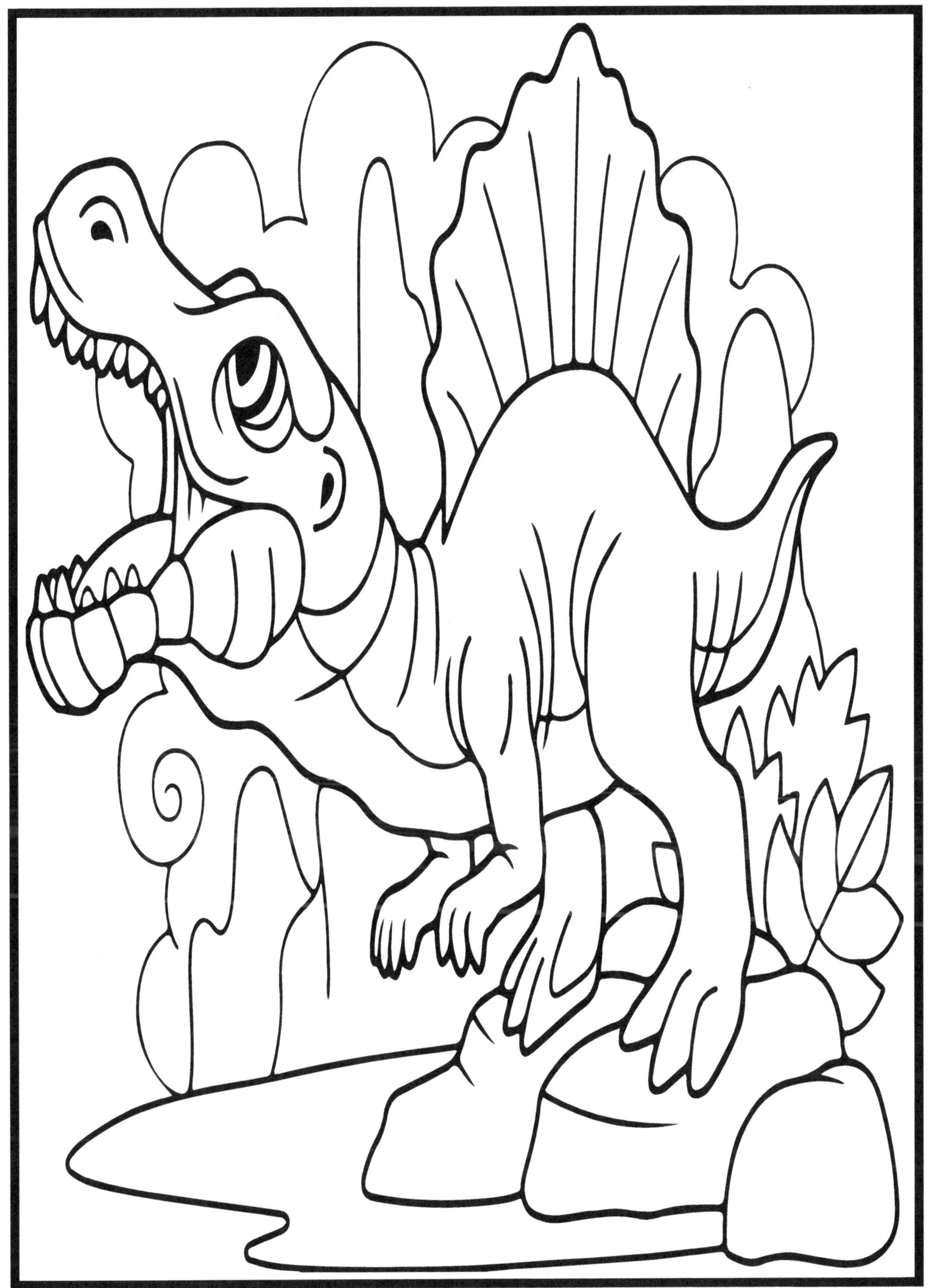

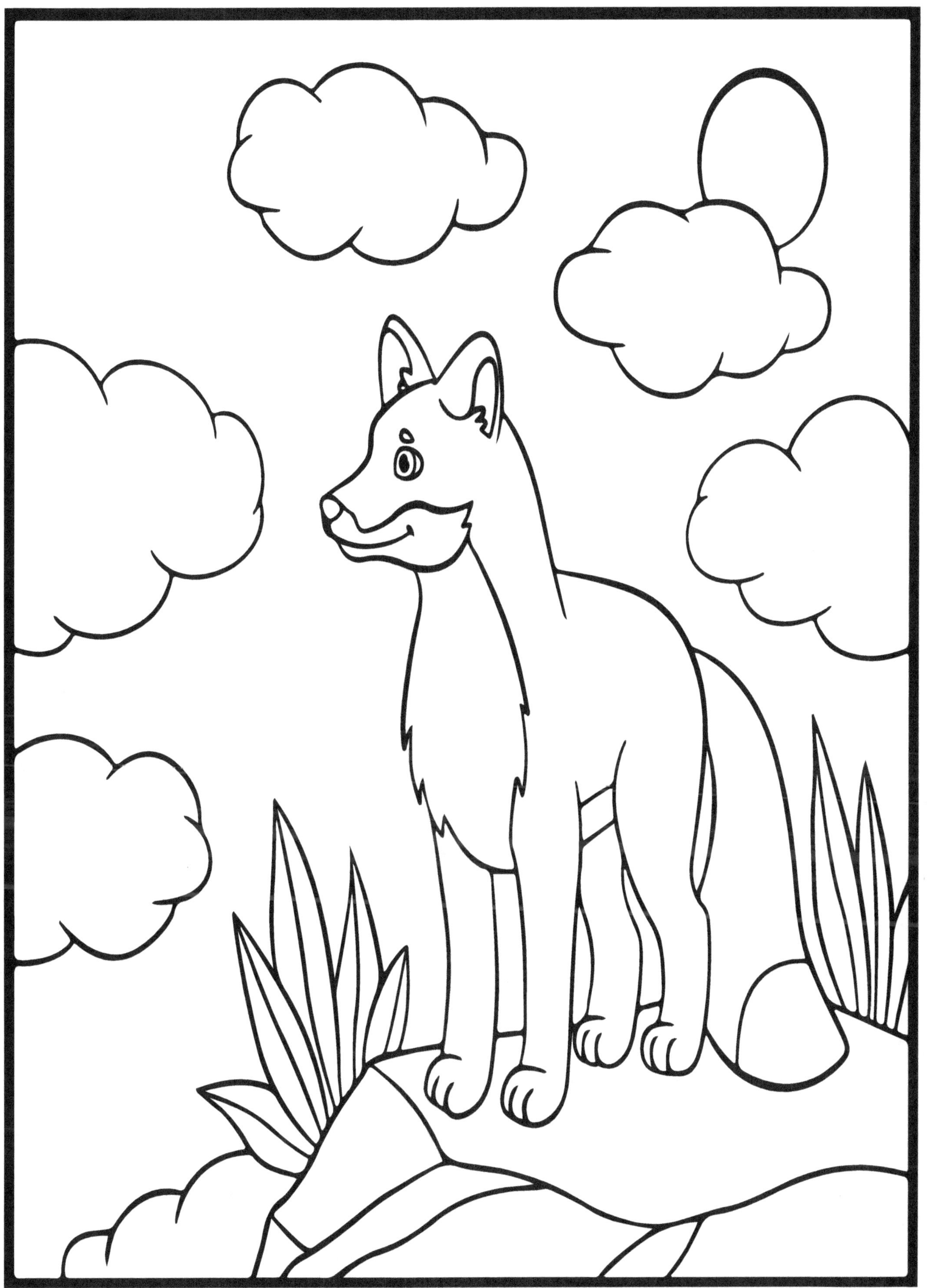

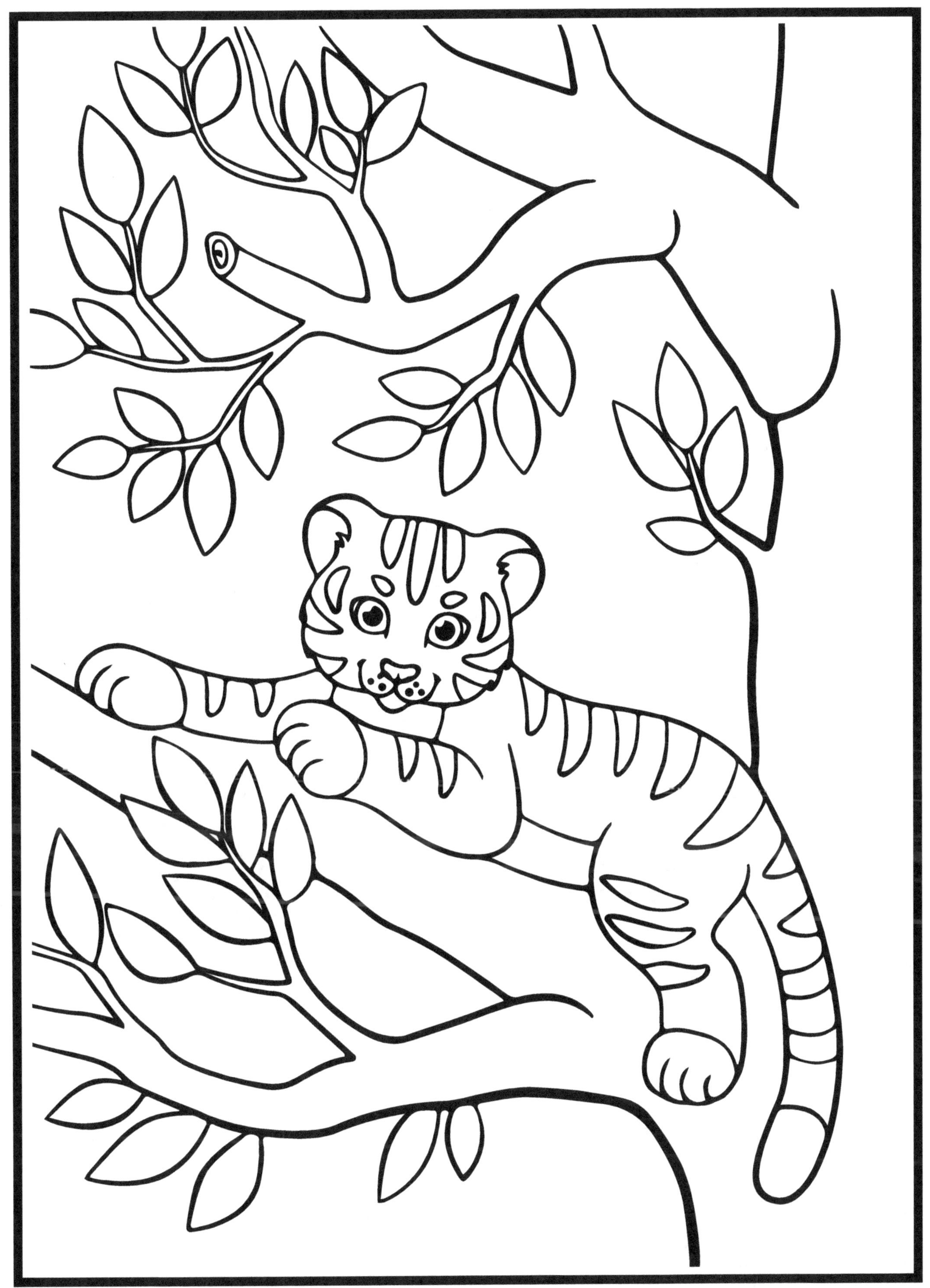

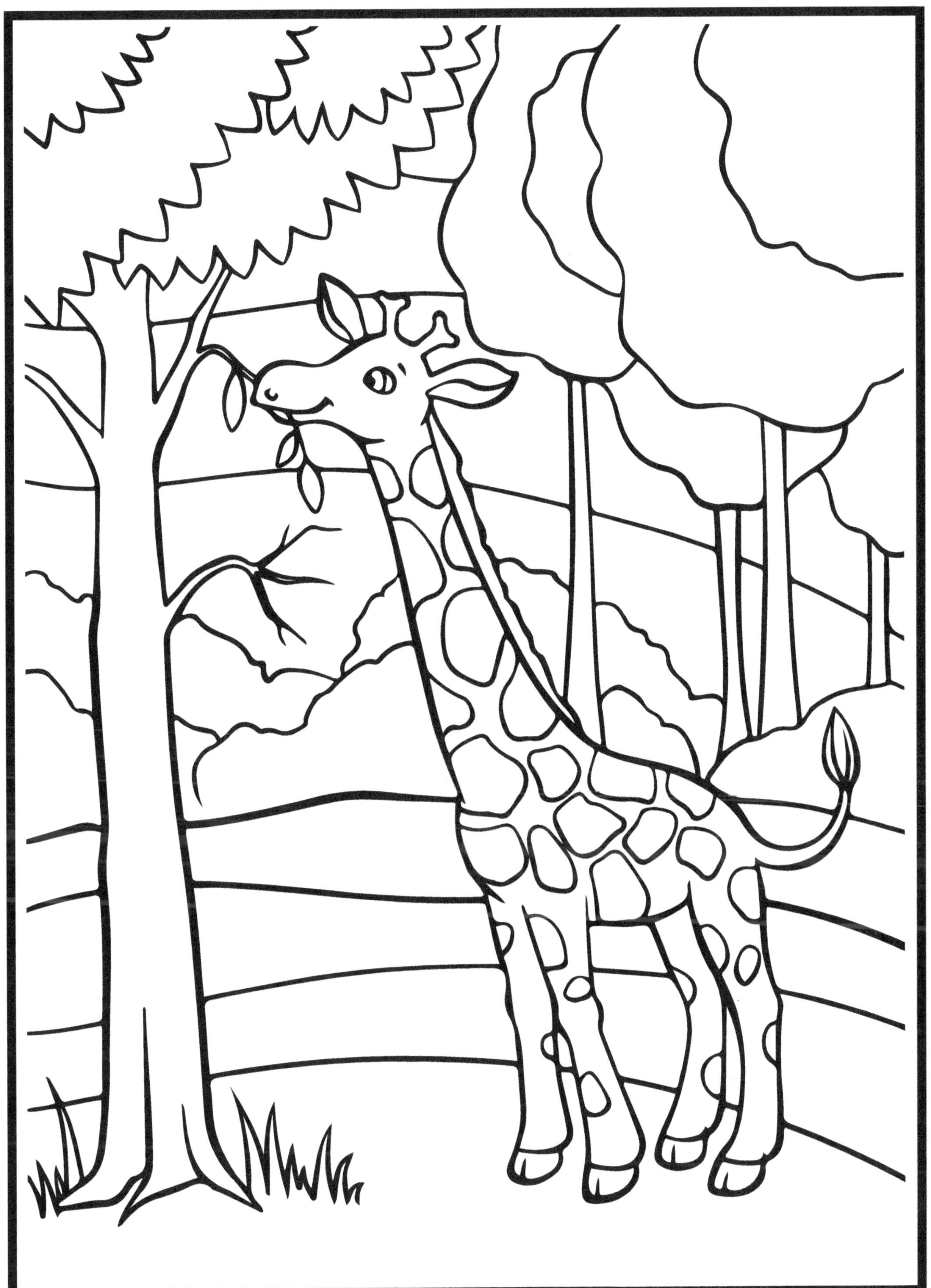

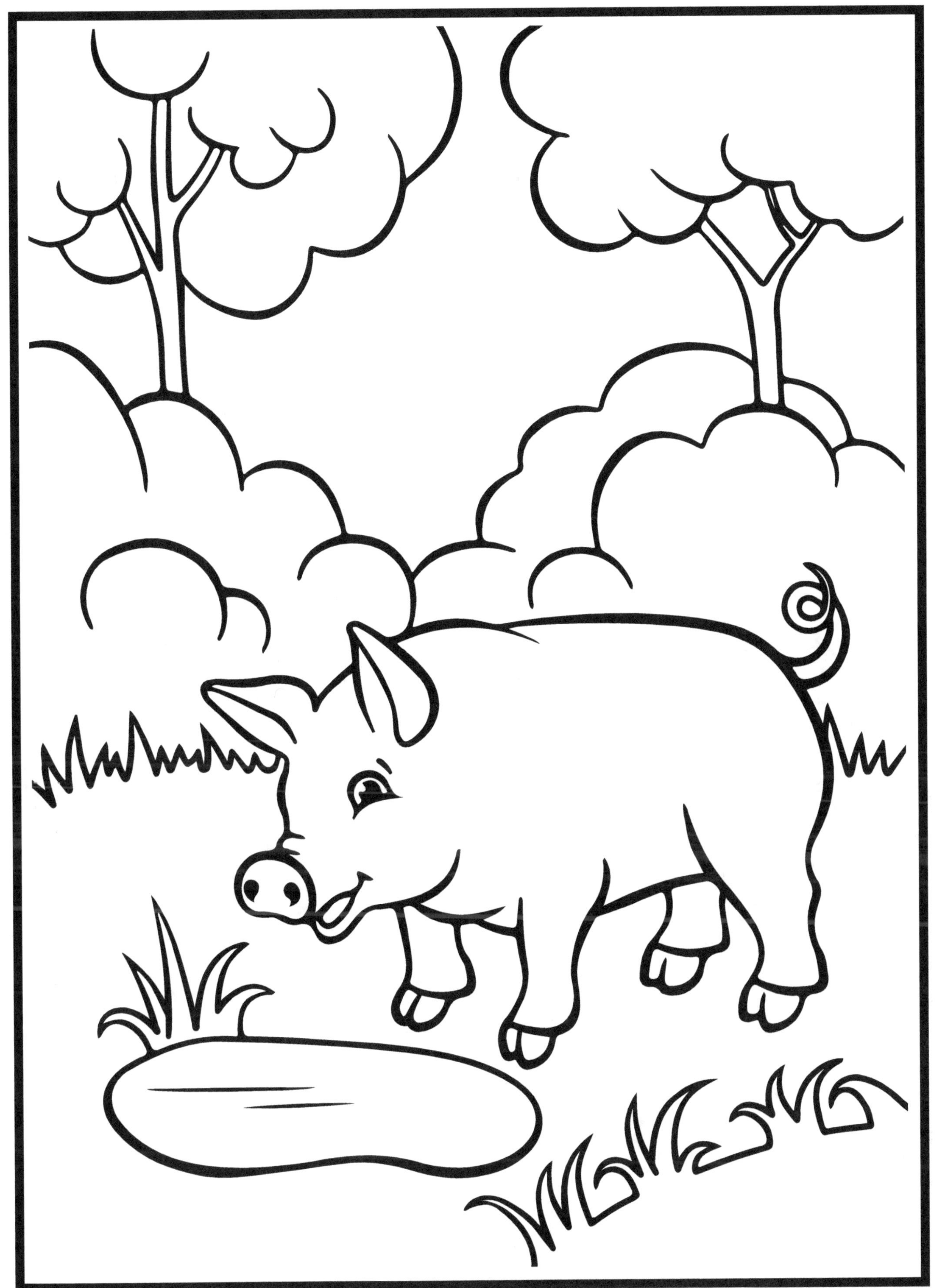

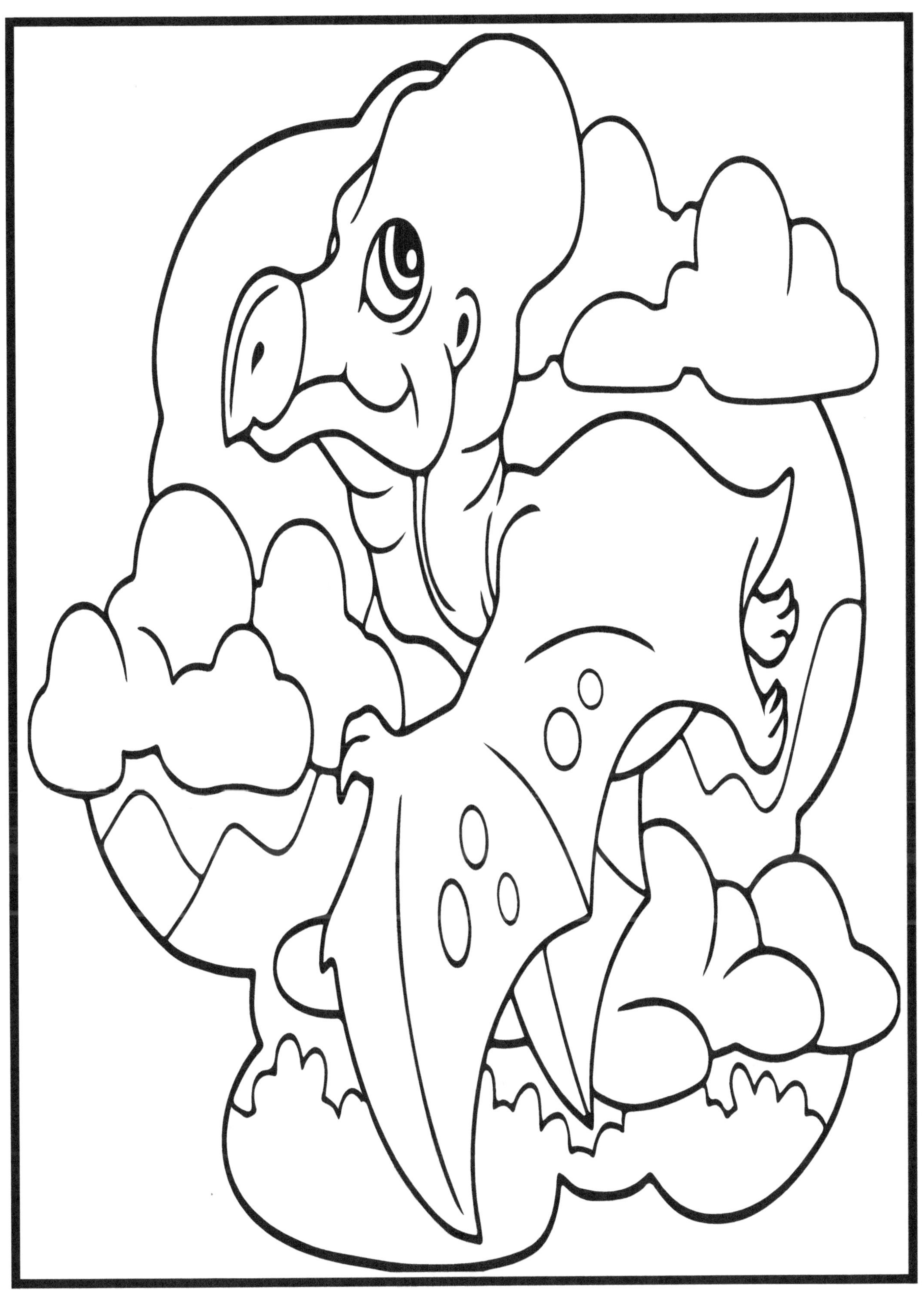

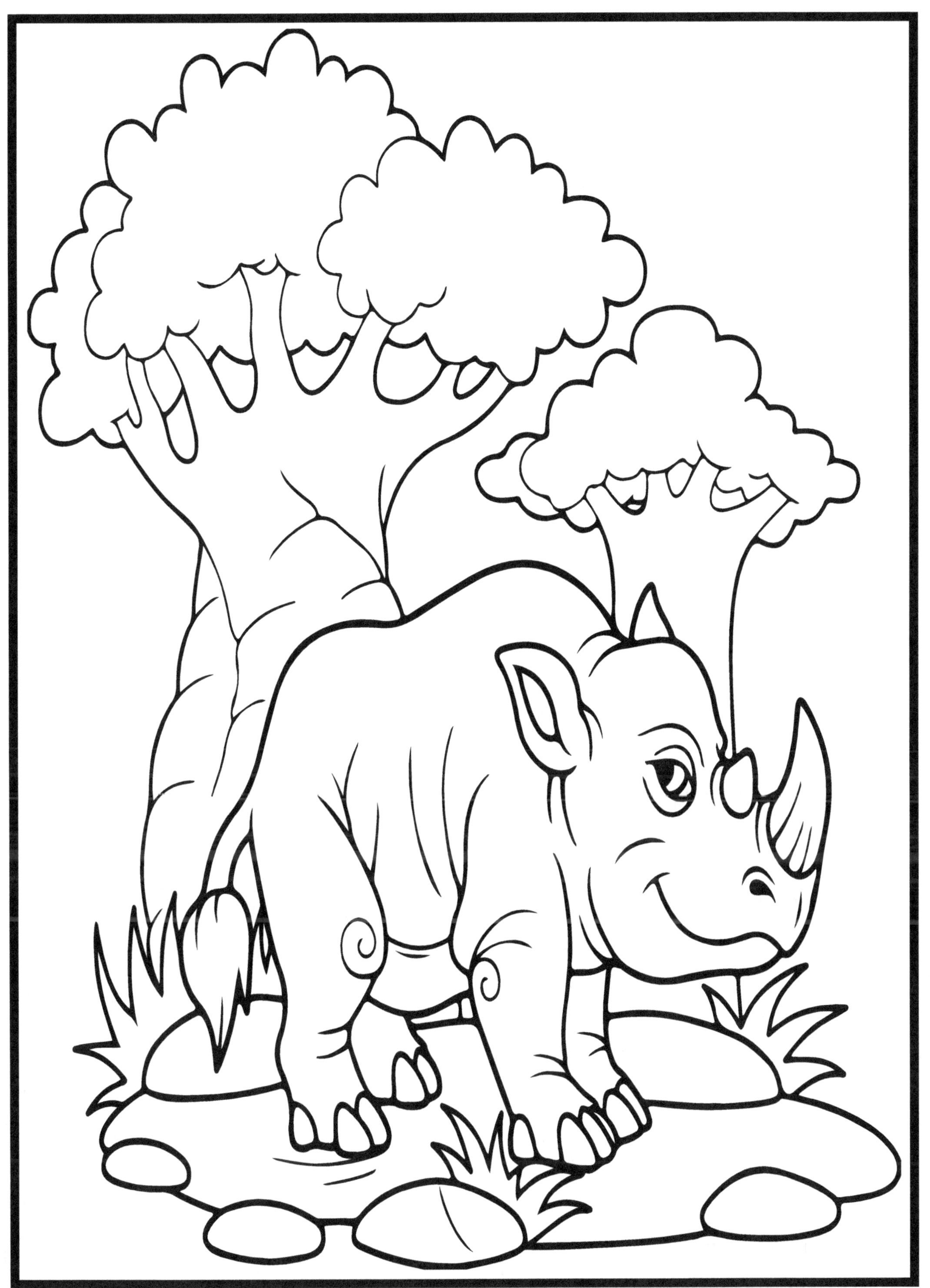

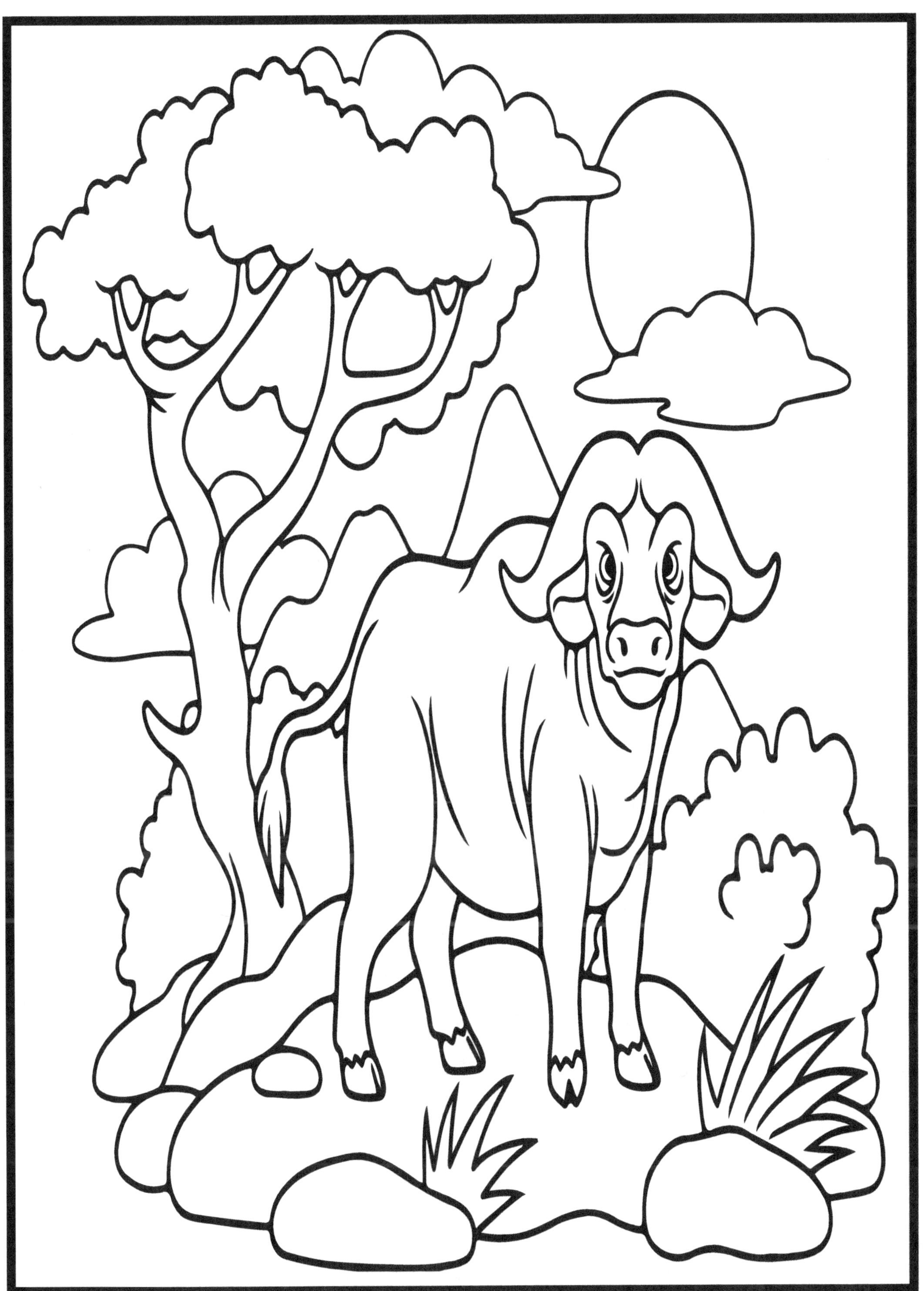

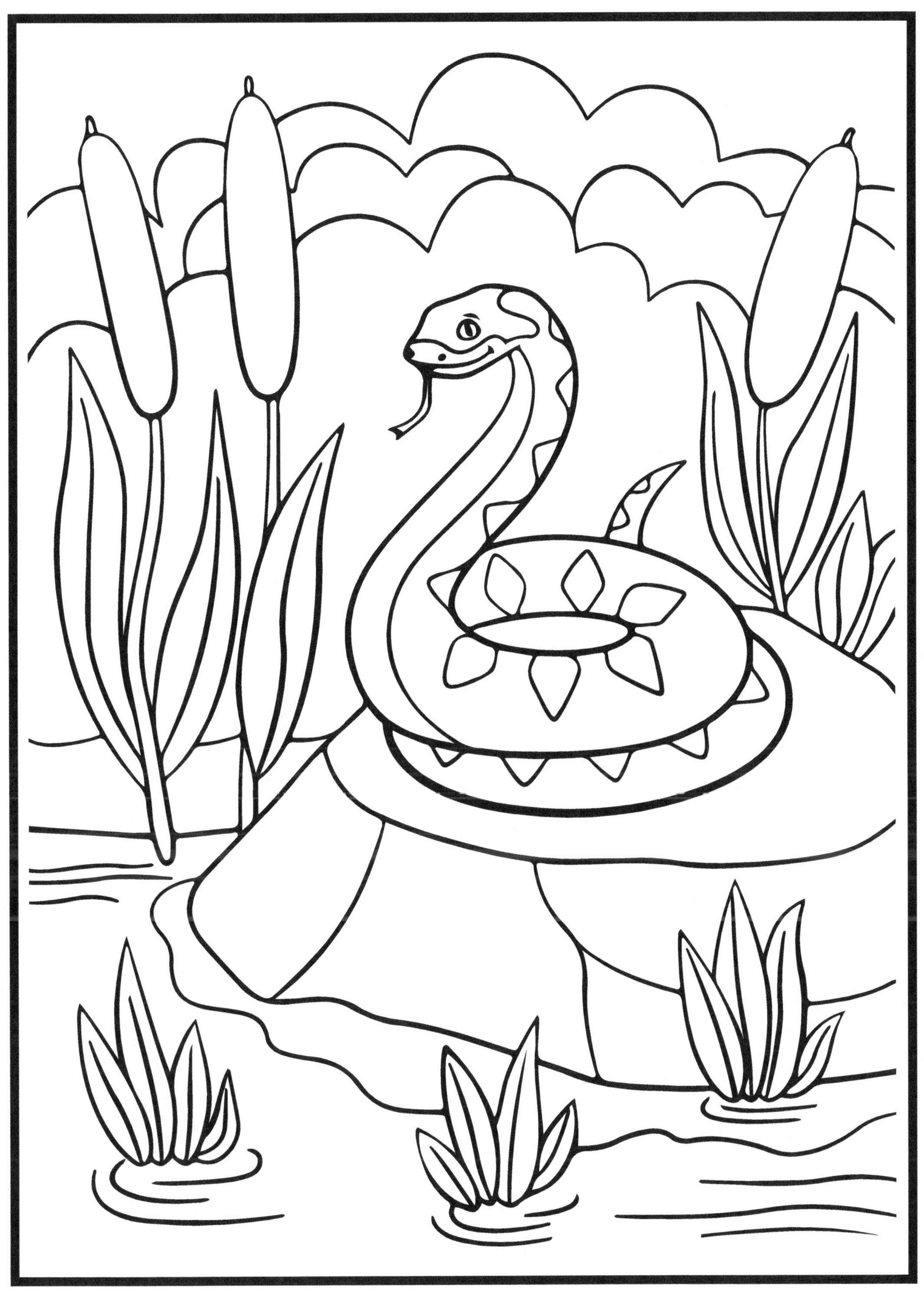

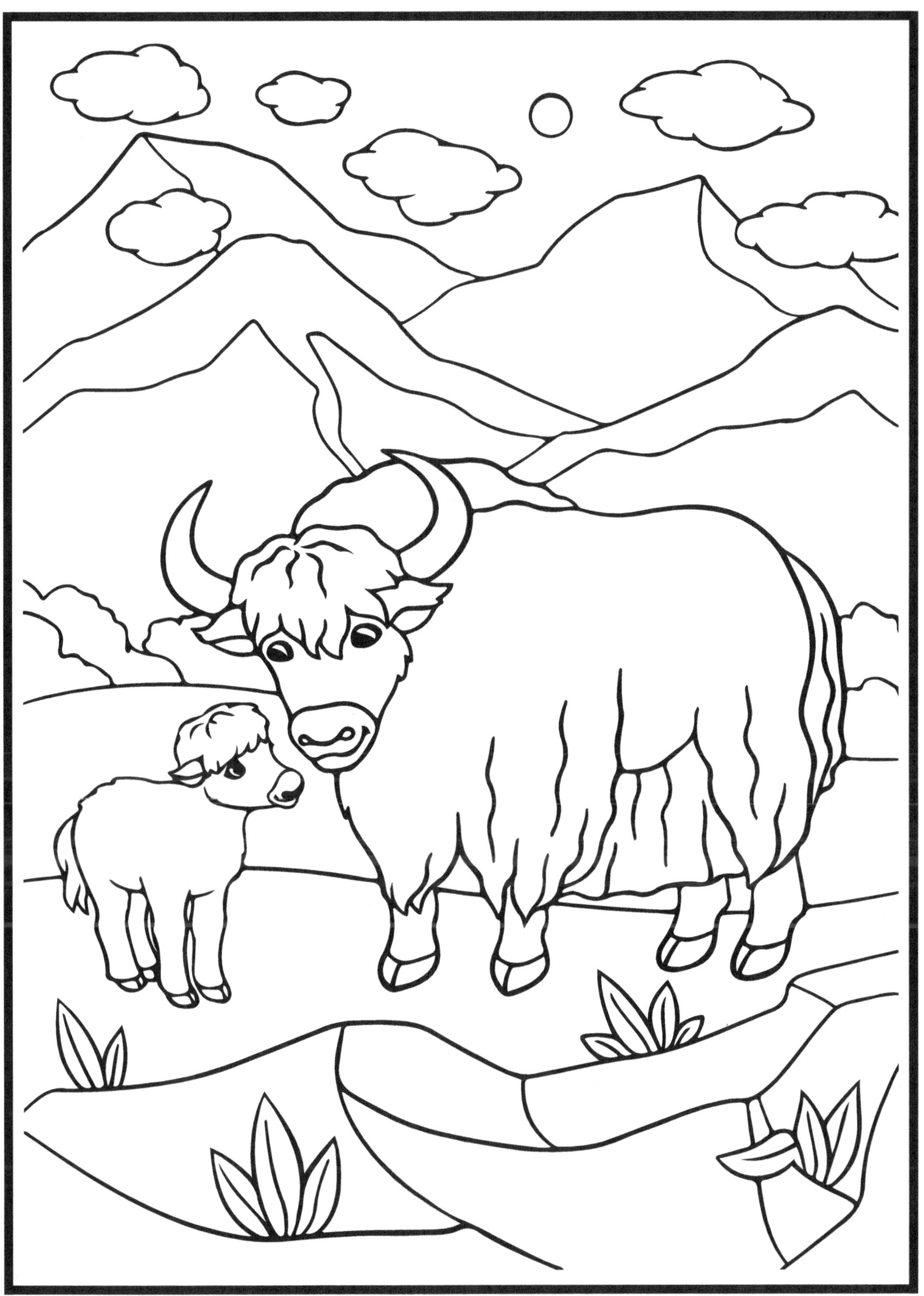

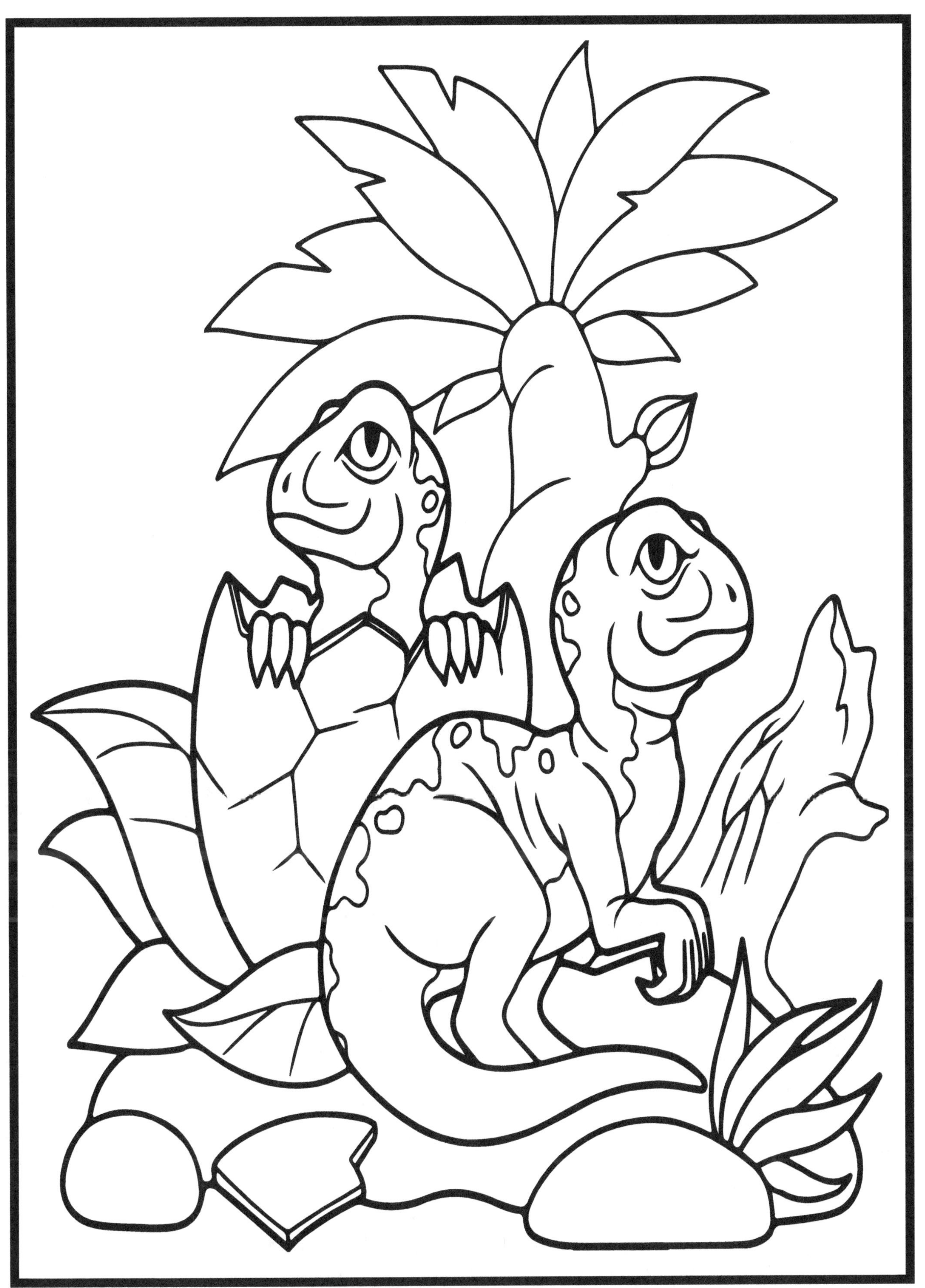

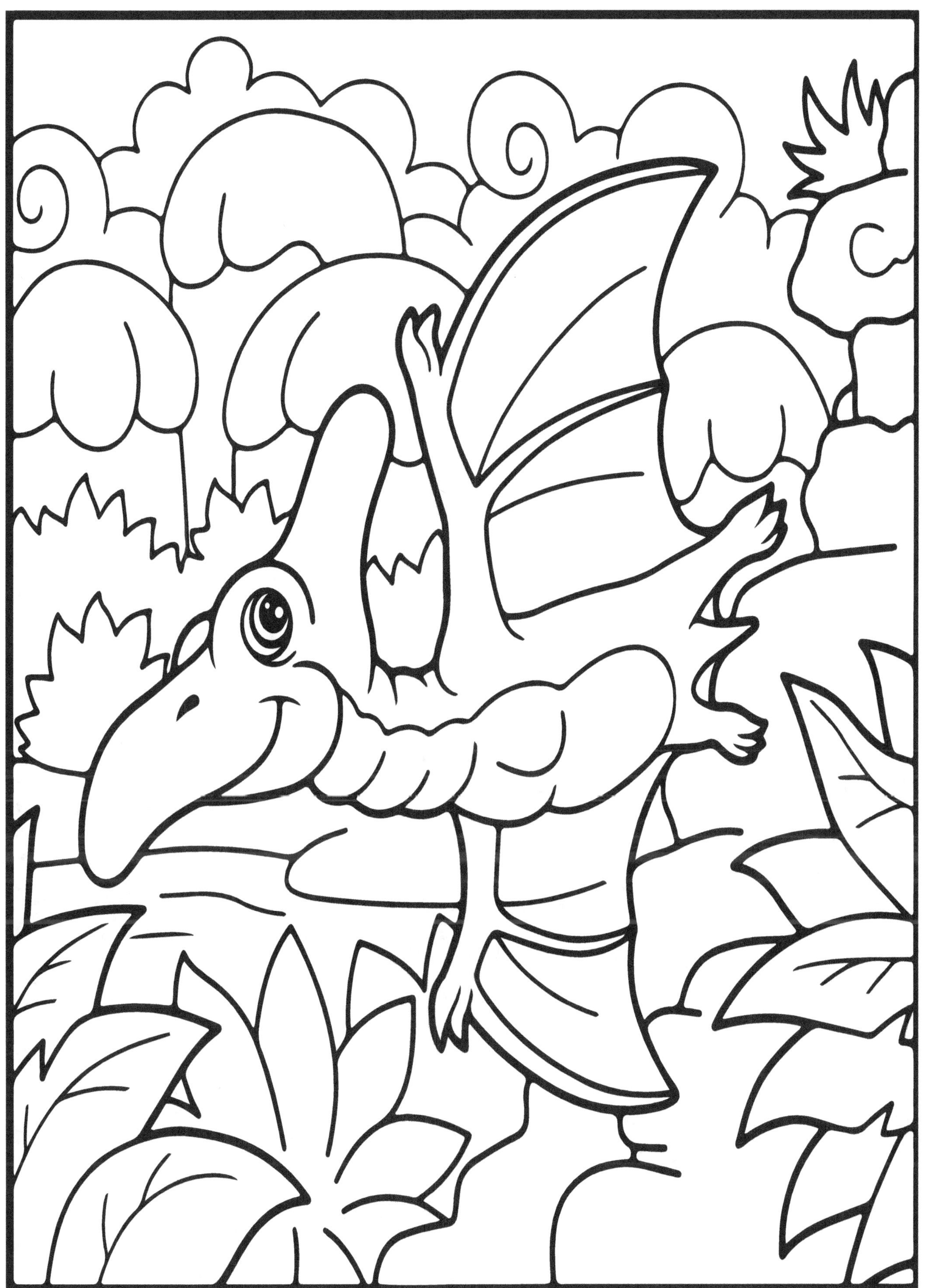

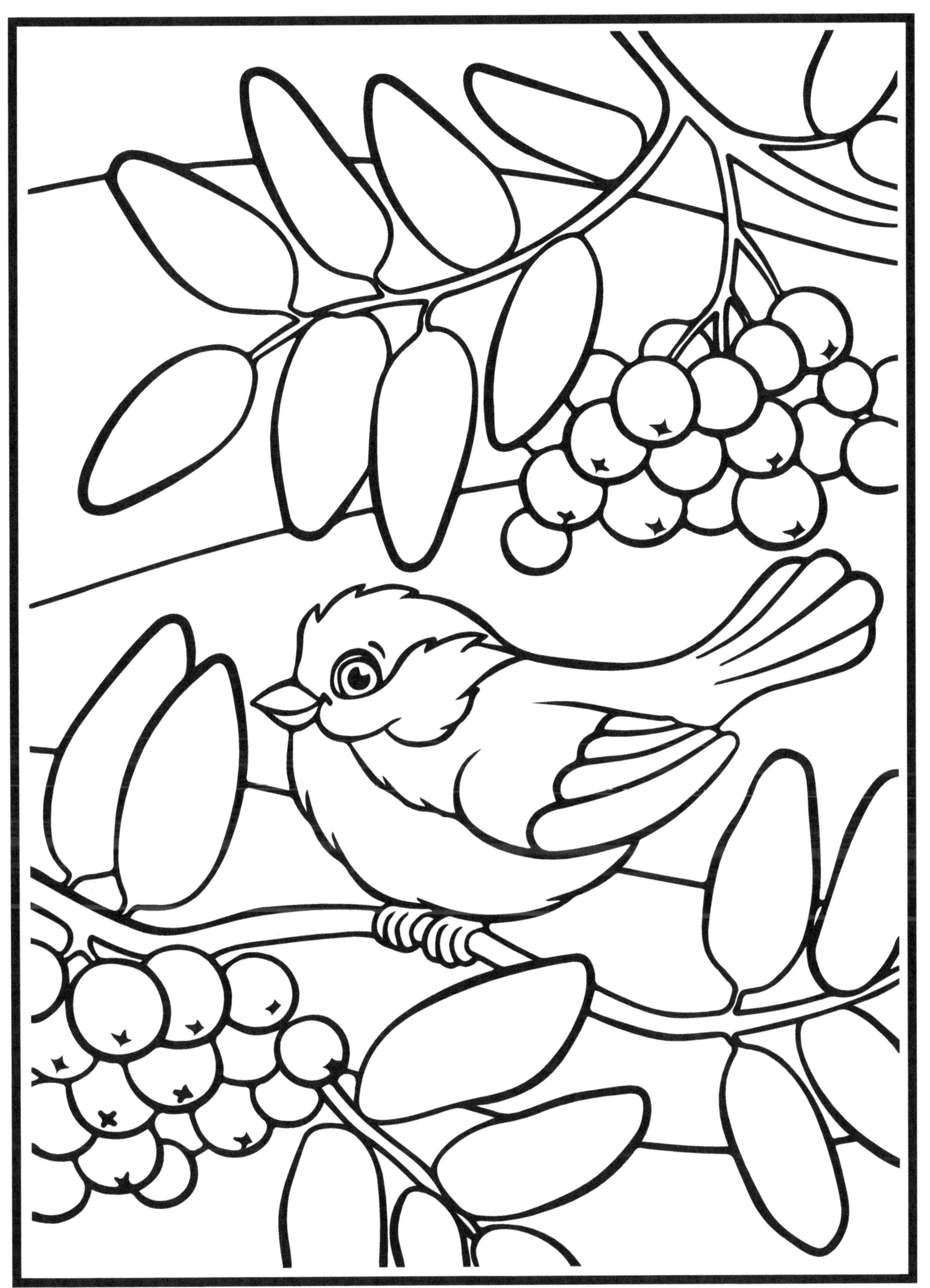

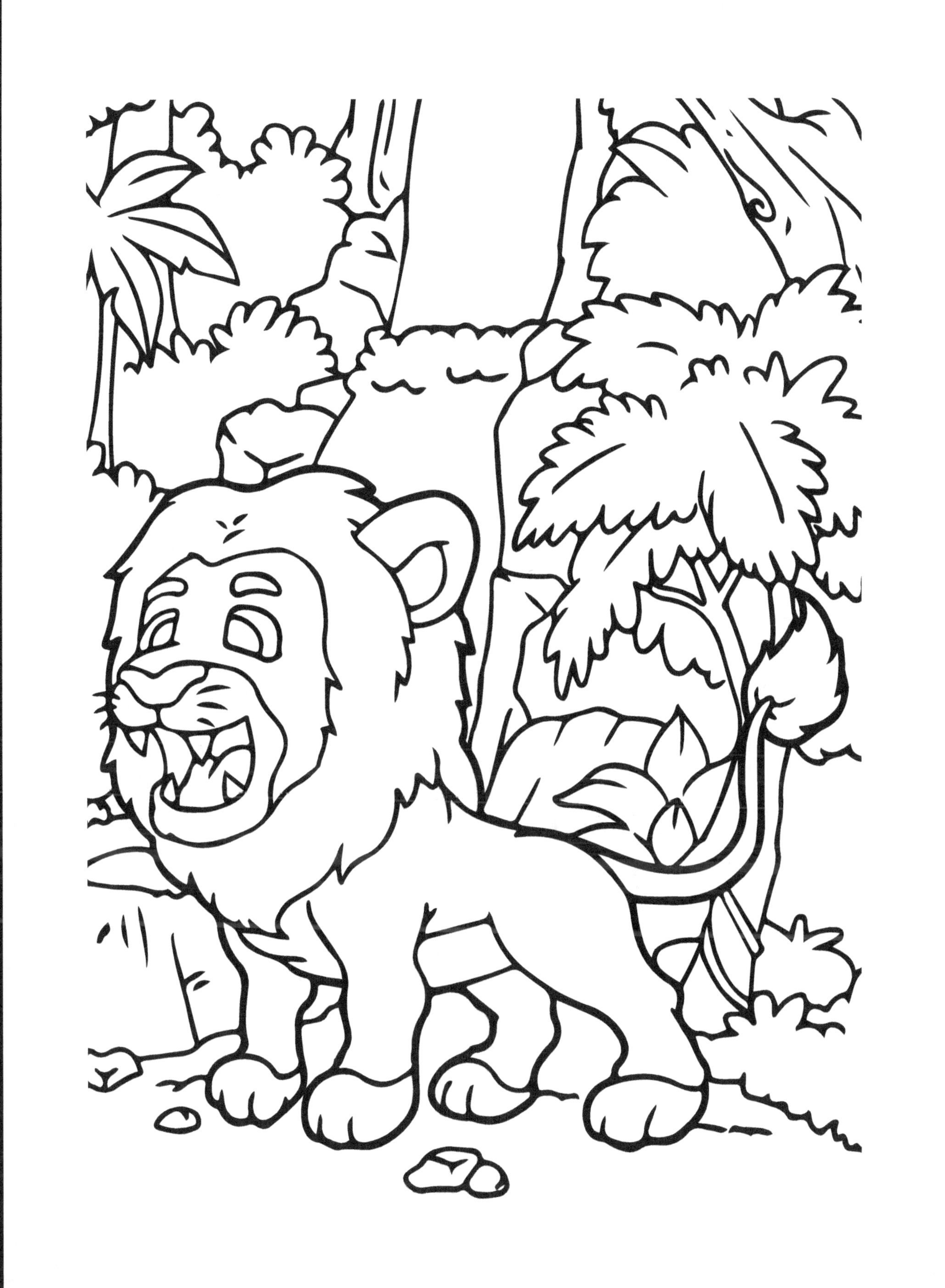

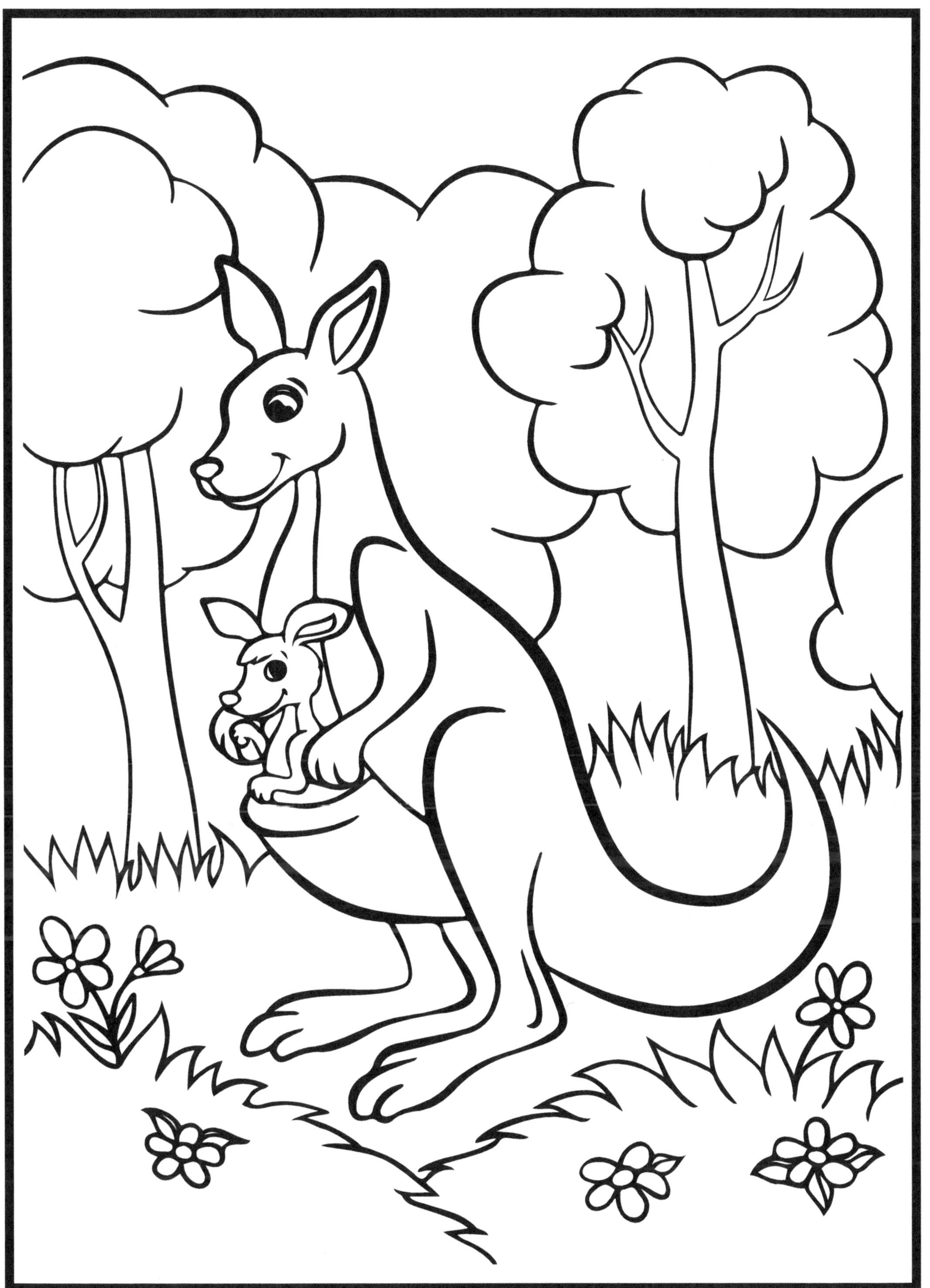